Myra L. Hidalgo, MSW

Sexual Abuse and the Culture of Catholicism

How Priests and Nuns Become Perpetrators

Pre-publication REVIEWS, COMMENTARIES, EVALUATIONS . . .

"This book goes far beyond the child sex abuse crisis by also examining sexual exploitation of adults by clergy, a topic often forgotten amidst the current scandals. Quite noteworthy is Hidalgo's observation that systematic sexual shame as taught by the church is part of the basis for sexual misconduct. Ironically, as the church is currently being shamed for the misconduct to some degree this cycle is continued. Unlike so many books on this topic, this is not about demons in the ranks of priests or nuns, but rather about social forces inside a faith that help shape the exploitation and abuse of parishioners and others. The author believes this book is just about Catholicism—I disagree. It is about the risks in all faith groups, and for that matter other organizations."

Gary R. Schoener
Clinical Psychologist,
Executive Director, Walk-In Counseling Center, Mpls

"This book is a useful tool for those readers interested in the intersection between clinical social work and religion, particularly the modern decades-old pedophilia scandal in the Roman Catholic Church. It is solidly referenced on the related problems of incest, child abuse, 'families of faith,' and sexually errant leaders. The author is admirably open about her motives for writing such a book as a former victim exploring the roots of her own victimology and the search for personal closure. Her work joins a growing corpus by critics both inside and outside the Catholic Church who by examining the dysfunctional system of rigid patriarchy and secrecy point to the structural remedies needed for healing."

Anson Shupe, PhD
Professor of Sociology,
Indiana University-Purdue University

More pre-publication
REVIEWS, COMMENTARIES, EVALUATIONS . . .

"Myra Hidalgo's book is one of the few that must be considered *foundational* for anyone seeking to understand how widespread sexual abuse and its cover-up by the hierarchy could be a part of the world's oldest and largest Christian denomination. This book makes a unique and essential contribution to the ongoing efforts to comprehend why Catholic clergy and nuns become sexual abusers and why the Church leadership has gone to such extraordinary lengths to cover this up. There are numerous 'new' insights and contributions in this book. Hidalgo's theory of clergy/religious sexual perpetration is certainly a major one and another is the manner with which she frames her goals in writing the book. The concluding 'implications for recovery, research, and prevention' are especially relevant because they relate the book's essential themes to practical steps that can be immediately taken by those willing to work at a basic change of attitude."

Thomas Patrick Doyle
Canon Lawyer; Author;
Researcher; Addictions Therapist;
Long-Time Clergy Abuse
Victim Advocate

The Haworth Maltreatment and Trauma Press®
An Imprint of The Haworth Press, Inc.
New York • London • Oxford

NOTES FOR PROFESSIONAL LIBRARIANS AND LIBRARY USERS

This is an original book title published by The Haworth Maltreatment and Trauma Press®, an Imprint of The Haworth Press, Inc. Unless otherwise noted in specific chapters with attribution, materials in this book have not been previously published elsewhere in any format or language.

CONSERVATION AND PRESERVATION NOTES

All books published by The Haworth Press, Inc., and its imprints are printed on certified pH neutral, acid-free book grade paper. This paper meets the minimum requirements of American National Standard for Information Sciences-Permanence of Paper for Printed Material, ANSI Z39.48-1984.

DIGITAL OBJECT IDENTIFIER (DOI) LINKING

The Haworth Press is participating in reference linking for elements of our original books. (For more information on reference linking initiatives, please consult the CrossRef Web site at www.crossref.org.) When citing an element of this book such as a chapter, include the element's Digital Object Identifier (DOI) as the last item of the reference. A Digital Object Identifier is a persistent, authoritative, and unique identifier that a publisher assigns to each element of a book. Because of its persistence, DOIs will enable The Haworth Press and other publishers to link to the element referenced, and the link will not break over time. This will be a great resource in scholarly research.

Sexual Abuse and the Culture of Catholicism

How Priests and Nuns Become Perpetrators

The Haworth Maltreatment and Trauma Press®
Maltreatment, Trauma, and Interpersonal Aggression
Robert A. Geffner
Senior Editor

Identifying Child Molesters: Preventing Child Sexual Abuse by Recognizing the Patterns of the Offenders by Carla van Dam

Patterns of Child Abuse: How Dysfunctional Transactions are Replicated in Individuals, Families, and the Child Welfare System by Michael Karson

Growing Free: A Manual for Survivors of Domestic Violence by Wendy Susan Deaton and Michael Hertica

We Are Not Alone: A Guidebook for Helping Professionals and Parents Supporting Adolescent Victims of Sexual Abuse by Jade Christine Angelica

We Are Not Alone: A Teenage Girl's Personal Account of Incest from Disclosure Through Prosecution and Treatment by Jade Christine Angelica

We Are Not Alone: A Teenage Boy's Personal Account of Child Sexual Abuse from Disclosure Through Prosecution and Treatment by Jade Christine Angelica

The Insiders: A Man's Recovery from Traumatic Childhood Abuse by Robert Blackburn Knight

Simple and Complex Post-Traumatic Stress Disorder: Strategies for Comprehensive Treatment in Clinical Practice edited by Mary Beth Williams and John F. Sommer Jr.

Child Maltreatment Risk Assessments: An Evaluation Guide by Sue Righthand, Bruce Kerr, and Kerry Drach

Mother-Daughter Incest: A Guide for Helping Professionals by Beverly A. Ogilvie

Munchausen by Proxy Maltreatment: Identification, Intervention, and Case Management by Louisa J. Lasher and Mary S. Sheridan

Effects of and Interventions for Childhood Trauma from Infancy Through Adolescence: Pain Unspeakable by Sandra B. Hutchison

The Socially Skilled Child Molester: Differentiating the Guilty from the Falsely Accused by Carla van Dam

Child Trauma Handbook: A Guide for Helping Trauma-Exposed Children and Adolescents by Ricky Greenwald

A Safe Place to Grow: A Group Treatment Manual for Children in Conflicted, Violent, and Separating Homes by Vivienne Roseby, Janet Johnston, Bettina Gentner, and Erin Moore

Overcoming Child Sexual Trauma: A Guide to Breaking Through the Wall of Fear for Practitioners and Survivors by Sheri Oz and Sarah-Jane Ogiers

Sexual Abuse and the Culture of Catholicism: How Priests and Nuns Become Perpetrators by Myra L. Hidalgo

Sexual Abuse and the Culture of Catholicism

How Priests and Nuns Become Perpetrators

Myra L. Hidalgo, MSW

The Haworth Maltreatment and Trauma Press®
An Imprint of The Haworth Press, Inc.
New York • London • Oxford

For more information on this book or to order, visit
http://www.haworthpress.com/store/product.asp?sku=5633

or call 1-800-HAWORTH (800-429-6784) in the United States and Canada
or (607) 722-5857 outside the United States and Canada

or contact orders@HaworthPress.com

Published by

The Haworth Maltreatment and Trauma Press®, an imprint of The Haworth Press, Inc., 10 Alice Street, Binghamton, NY 13904-1580.

Identities and circumstances of individuals discussed in this book have been changed to protect confidentiality.

Cover design by Jennifer M. Gaska.

Library of Congress Cataloging-in-Publication Data

Hidalgo, Myra L.
Sexual abuse and the culture of Catholicism : how priests and nuns become perpetrators / Myra L. Hidalgo.
p. cm.
Includes bibliographical references.
ISBN-13: 978-0-7890-2955-3 (hard 13 : alk. paper)
ISBN-10: 0-7890-2955-3 (hard 10 : alk. paper)
ISBN-13: 978-0-7890-2956-0 (soft 13 : alk. paper)
ISBN-10: 0-7890-2956-1 (soft 10 : alk. paper)
1. Catholic Church—Clergy—Sexual behavior. 2. Nuns—Sexual behavior. 3. Child sexual abuse by clergy. 4. Child sexual abuse—Religious aspects—Catholic Church. I. Title.

BX1912.9.H53 2007
261.8'3272088282—dc22

2006034697

This book is dedicated
to all who have experienced
religious-based sexual trauma
and to the therapists who help us heal.

ABOUT THE AUTHOR

Myra L. Hidalgo, MSW, operates a private psychotherapy practice in New Orleans, Louisiana, and holds a position as adjunct faculty at Tulane University School of Social Work. Ms. Hidalgo is pursuing a PhD in social work at Louisiana State University in Baton Rouge; her areas of special interest include child sexual abuse and gay, lesbian, bisexual, and transgender issues. She is the co-founder of ANSWERS on www.AbuseByNuns.com, an Internet-based support and information service on the issue of sexual abuse and exploitation by women religious.

CONTENTS

Foreword

Since the mid-1980s the Catholic Church has been rocked by repeated revelations of sexual abuse by its clergy. Perpetrators included deacons, priests, bishops, and at least one cardinal. Although the initial public revelations captured media attention in 1984, the uncovering of a massive cover-up by *The Boston Globe* in January 2002 thrust the issue onto center stage, where it remained for over a year. More than four years have passed and the victims of Catholic clergy sexual abuse continue to come forward. Their cases plod on in the civil courts and the Catholic hierarchy continues to defend its indefensible actions.

The phenomenon of clergy sexual abuse was first described as a "crisis" and has been regularly referred to as a "scandal." Though the revelations since the mid-1980s have shocked many, the historical reality is that sexual misconduct and violations of mandatory celibacy by Catholic clerics and religious women is not new in our era. The Catholic Church's own official documentation shows a regular pattern of awareness of sexual abuse and consistent attempts to curb it and enforce celibacy through disciplinary measures. What we have

---

Father Thomas Doyle is a Dominican priest with a doctorate in canon law and certification as an addictive disorders counselor. He became an expert on the problem of sexual abuse in the Catholic Church during the time he served as a canon lawyer for the Vatican Embassy in Washington, DC, from 1981 to 1986. At that time, a number of accusations of child abuse by priests, bishops, and members of religious orders were reported to the embassy. Fr. Doyle has since become a major advocate for victims of clerical sex abuse and has received numerous awards for his work including the Cavallo Award for Moral Courage in 1992, the Priest of Integrity Award from Voice of the Faithful in 2002, and the Isaac Hecker Award from the Paulist Fathers in 2003. He has published extensively on the topic of sexual abuse in the Catholic Church and recently co-authored the book *Sex, Priests, and Secret Codes: The Catholic Church's 2,000-Year Paper Trail of Sexual Abuse* (Volt Press, 2006).

Sexual Abuse and the Culture of Catholicism

doi:10.1300/5633_a

seen in the past two decades is neither an acute crisis nor a passing scandal. Rather, it is evidence of a strain of toxicity that remains deeply embedded in institutionalized Catholicism and in the clerical elite that governs the Church and controls its relationships with secular society.

The Church's leadership managed to keep sexual abuse of the vulnerable by its clerics and nuns a deeply buried secret until the secular media and the civil justice system forced the painful exposures we are seeing. The institutional Church, from the Vatican down to the local level, has consistently reacted in a defensive manner that has exposed the scandalous reality of the hierarchy being obsessed with its image and power and hardly concerned about the welfare of its victims. There is no evidence of a serious commitment to delve into the complex existential reality of institutionalized sexual abuse to find out why it is happening now and why it has remained a part of the Catholic clerical culture for centuries.

This has been the Catholic Church's worst nightmare. Rather than look to the many available resources in secular society for answers to the constant stream of painful questions that will not go away, the Church's hierarchical leadership remains stuck in a narcissistic sinkhole. The avalanche of critical media coverage and the constant revelations of the heretofore buried shameful secrets through civil court processes have highlighted the toxic sense of corporate entitlement and arrogance of a worldwide organization that has acted more like a threatened business empire than a Christian church. The Church has been *forced* to respond and to look within. It has not done so voluntarily with a spirit of openness, admission of responsibility, and respect for the countless victims whose lives have been devastated. The well-known reports of the National Review Board, the John Jay College of Criminal Justice, and the Gavin Group have provided some valuable information, but can hardly be considered the definitive response to the pressing need for complete answers to a vexing phenomenon that has devastated the spiritual and emotional lives of millions.

While the institutional leadership of the Catholic Church and the clerical subculture that comprises this leadership has remained on the defensive, scholars from a multitude of related disciplines have forged ahead, looking for plausible reasons why the world's largest and oldest religious denomination could stand for goodness, compassion, and justice in its official pronouncements and at the same time allow the continued pathological strain of behavior that contradicts everything for which the Church purports to stand.

None of the answers offered by the institutional Church and its apologists has amounted to anything more than superficial excuses that lack honesty, insight, and depth. Among other things, the hierarchy, guided by their secular public relations specialists, has appealed to purported scientific studies in an attempt to minimize the abuse problem and to isolate it as an anomaly or temporary distraction from the Church's true nature. At the same time, the Catholic leadership from the Vatican to the National Conference of Catholic Bishops has resisted offers from scholars to study the wealth of data gathered by therapists who have worked with both perpetrators and victims, and it has outright forbidden any objective studies of the impact of mandatory celibacy.

True progress is being made by scholars in the social and behavioral sciences as well as by Church theologians and historians who are not hampered by official Church censorship. The most effective responses to the revelations of sexual abuse and institutional cover-up and deception are not polemic and combative but scholarly and dispassionate. Such studies will separate the individuals in the institution's leadership roles and even the clergy and nun perpetrators from the sociocultural–theological system which perpetuated a way of life and manner of government that created and enabled systemic sexual abuse.

Myra Hidalgo's work is a foundational contribution to the scholarly efforts to find the reasons *why*. Her personal story, which had no small influence on her motivation to conduct the research that resulted in this book, is recounted with complete honesty and objectivity. The painstaking scholarship and research that is so obvious throughout this work is not grounded in anger or thirst for revenge. Rather, it reflects the commitment of a woman whose personal and professional life is inspired and guided by the motivation to aid in healing the deep and painful wounds of sexual abuse.

The Catholic Church uses language and symbology of the family to describe its structure and mission. The pope is known as the "Holy Father." The Church is commonly referred to as "Holy Mother Church," and the clergy and male and female religious are officially addressed as Father, Brother, or Sister. Myra Hidalgo applies a realistic and insightful systems approach to lay the groundwork for the conclusions of her scholarship. She builds a solid foundation for the proposition that the Church is a sexually abusive family. But *why* is this so?

One can hardly look at the viral effects of sexually abusive clerics and religious without arriving at the center of the concentric circles of pathology, and in that center is found the hierarchical leadership. Hidalgo is correct in her assessment of the anachronistic, patriarchal governmental system and its reliance on an antediluvian philosophy of human sexuality as the probable reasons why the Church's leadership has consistently dismissed contemporary social and behavioral scientific advances, especially in this realm of sexuality. The elders of this dysfunctional family have routinely responded to the complex pathology not with support for research leading to insights that might help heal the massive wound but with one defensive word, *Obey!*

The author makes significant headway in the search for answers by focusing on shame as an authentic source of sexual trauma. This shame is a natural outcome of "rigid, conservative, religious, and cultural beliefs" (Hidalgo, p. 88). Catholic sexual philosophy has dominated its teaching about male-female relationships, gender issues, marriage, homosexuality, and clerical celibacy. This view of sexuality has been two dimensional: cognitive and volitional. According to the Church, all expressions of sexuality are reserved for married men and women. Sexuality has not been seen as an integral part of the human person. It is as if the nonmarried, especially celibate clerics, are expected to live as if their sexuality were a component of their personhood that is detached from them. In order to maintain the illusion that such separation is indeed possible, a guilt-inducing rigid belief system was used to control clerics and lay persons alike. The institutionalized shaming has had a profound impact on many sexually dysfunctional clerics as well as on their victims.

The author credibly ties together many disparate elements of the complex reality of clergy and religious sexual abuse: risk factors in perpetrators, problems with therapeutic recovery for victims, healing the "hidden wounded," and the ineffective responses by the hierarchy, to mention a few. She relates these to the basic concept of sexual trauma derived from the Church's traditional sexual teaching and philosophy. Her fundamental thesis about the future is this: The institutional Church's strategic, administrative response to the sexual abuse phenomenon will continue to be ineffective. Sexual abuse by clergy and religious is not the totality of the problem but a major symptom of a "systemic social dysfunction that has corrupted Catholicism over centuries through a cycle of systemic sexual trauma."

Thomas P. Doyle, JCD, CADC

Acknowledgments

In addition to the knowledgeable team of professionals at The Haworth Press, many people helped in various ways to make this book possible. I am indebted to the friends, colleagues, mentors, and family members who provided valuable advice and emotional support during the time of my decision to go public with my story and eventually to write this book. Included among these are Sister Carmelita Centanni, Noel Cieutat, Cathy Clancy, Rev. Tom Doyle, Robert Hayden, Cindy Heine, Sister Mary Kay Kinberger, Sarah Kreitziger, Rick Laskowski, Victoria McCardell, Gillian Perret, Louis Rom, Andrea Scheele, Chris South, Sister Sue Ellen Tennyson, Michael Zakour, and the Habits-of-Sin support group. I am especially grateful for the early encouragement of Katherine V. Forrest. Allison Blake was most important in the completion of this book. She offered an objective ear, critical feedback, and tireless editing advice throughout the writing process. Without her input, I never would have thought that I was capable of writing a book or that anyone would be interested in reading it.

There are dear friends, family members, and therapists who have played critical roles in getting me through the most difficult times in my life. I would especially like to acknowledge Joyce Beaugh, Gregory Darbonne, Carol Hidalgo, Andrea Izzo, Tom Perrault, Libby Tisdell, Debbie Villa, and Deedy Young for standing by me through the darkness until I could find my way back to light. Of particular importance in my personal recovery, in my development as a young adult, and throughout my struggle to make sense of the world and my life experiences was Marly Sweeney. She was not only a talented and patient therapist for me, but has been a wonderful role model, both personally and professionally.

Sexual Abuse and the Culture of Catholicism

doi:10.1300/5633_b

Finally, I am eternally grateful for the tremendous love, understanding, and unwavering support of my life partner, Amy Archinal, and our furry family. Amy has brought meaning and joy to my life that I never dreamed was possible. Special acknowledgment also goes to Mango, the perfect writer's dog—I will miss her always.

Introduction

As a clinical social worker, my greatest intention in writing this book is to contribute to the prevention of childhood sexual abuse, an issue that most professionals in the fields of mental health and social welfare recognize as a major contributor to a wide variety of chronic psychiatric disturbances and related social problems. The second intention is to bridge the gaps between multiple perspectives on this multifaceted issue of sexual abuse in the Roman Catholic Church. Victim advocates and survivors of sexual abuse by priests and nuns have focused on a need for the validation of their horrific experiences and a restoration of personal power. The Catholic laity has demanded greater accountability from their bishops, while ecclesiastics have been concerned with protecting the traditions and teachings of the institutional church. Other Catholics, struggling to keep their faith, have mourned the harm done in the name of their church. Meanwhile, behavioral scientists have been concerned with identifying, treating, and preventing abuse by clergy and other religious offenders. I can appreciate each of these perspectives, and so I hope that this book will highlight the full scope of this crisis.

My most pressing reason for writing this book, however, is more personal. Once a devout Catholic, who is now estranged from the Church, I hold a strong motivation to influence reform and to promote healing for all who have been affected by sexual trauma in the Catholic Church. What lies beneath this passion is a personal struggle to resolve my own traumatic experiences related to childhood sexual abuse at the hands of a Catholic nun. This book is a result of my quest for a deeper understanding of how this abuse could have happened to me as a youth and to so many others raised in the Catholic faith. What contributed to our trusted teachers, mentors, and spiritual role models becoming sexual predators? How is it that neither our families nor the

Sexual Abuse and the Culture of Catholicism

doi:10.1300/5633_c

Church community were able to protect us? What role did our Catholic beliefs about sexuality and authority play in making us vulnerable to abuse? What factors might explain how this whole crisis of sexual abuse by priests and nuns came to be? I hope, now, that through my own attempt to answer these questions, I can contribute to a more enlightened approach as attempts to solve the problem of sexual abuse in the Catholic Church are made.

As with all researchers, I approach my topic with both expertise based on individualized professional knowledge and bias due to subjective experience. My biases may be more or less apparent to the reader, but each influences my perspective in ways that I hope are more enlightening than obscuring. Though I have tried to control the limiting effects of personal bias in my writing, it is impossible for anyone to fully escape the confines of subjective human perception. Thus, in the interest of truth and credibility, I shall attempt to explicate my biases along with my unique qualifications for writing this book.

As a victim or survivor, I cannot help but discuss this topic with a desire to feel personally validated and empowered through revealing my experience in a way that generates respect. This desire reflects a common narcissistic defense for all victims of personal trauma spawned by a need to be reminded that it was not our fault. Of course, this bias was the primary source of my determination to include sexual abuse by women religious in my analysis of the crisis in the Church. However, this determination has been tempered by yet another bias I carry as a feminist on many social issues. While the feminist movement of the 1960s and 1970s is credited with raising awareness on the issues of sexual abuse and exploitation, it has also contributed to an unfortunate stereotype of victims as always female and perpetrators as always male. At times, it has been difficult even for me to acknowledge that women are capable of horrendous acts of sexual aggression and that boys and men are also vulnerable to abuse.

Another personal attribute that lends itself to bias is my identity and status as an "out" lesbian in a committed sexual relationship. The celebration of my sexuality and lifestyle certainly affects my perspective in questioning the role of homosexuality in my own abuse and in the vast majority of cases reported in the Church. The same degree of bias also exists for those who celebrate a heterosexual lifestyle, whether celibate or sexual, which appears to be the case for most other authors on this topic. My years of experience as a clinical director of a mental health center and a therapist specializing in treating gay, lesbian, bisexual, and transgender clients has added to my knowledge of psychosocial issues affecting sexual minority populations, including psychosexual disorders.

Similarly, through my history as a very devout Catholic, I can relate strongly to those faithful followers who felt appalled and betrayed by the lack of sensitivity and accountability of church officials who failed to act responsibly in addressing abuse allegations. Yet, through my experience as a supervisor of beginning therapists, I have come to appreciate that ethical decision making can often become muddied by competing demands for service and training and by previously unchallenged administrative norms.

All of my personal and professional experiences influence my perspective as an author on this topic through bias or expertise. However, I believe that the strongest influences on my current approach to this subject have been my disciplinary training as a social worker, my years of experience as a psychotherapist, and my commitment to promoting scholarly research.

The ultimate goal of this book is to shift attention in the Catholic Church sexual abuse scandal to a need for healing dialogue, further research, and informed prevention strategies. In an effort to restore their credibility in 2002, U.S. bishops and leaders of religious orders of men developed policies clarifying new norms and procedures for dealing with allegations of abuse as they are reported. They created independent review panels to oversee the implementation of these new policies and to collect data on the number and nature of allegations that were reported. Meanwhile, victim advocates have focused primarily on compensatory rights of victims and punitive sanctions against abusive clergy and their bishops. None of these approaches, however, is aimed at preventing situations of sexual abuse from developing in the first place. In the past ten years, prevention strategies have included screening procedures at seminaries and convents and religious formation classes in human sexuality. Although these efforts are certainly notable, they are not based on evidence from research that would indicate their efficacy. At best, they are sincere efforts based on a limited view of the problem and unsupported speculation about its causes. At worst, they are politically motivated efforts to promote specific agendas and minimize legal risk.

Despite the scandals of the past three decades, church leaders have shrewdly avoided any meaningful investigation into the underlying causes of sexual exploitation by Catholic priests and religious. They continue to deny or minimize the range and extent of sexual exploitation practiced within church walls. For the most part, they have ignored sexual abuse perpetrated by women religious, instead deflecting responsibility to ill-prepared congregational leaders.

In response to public debate about factors contributing to the abuse crisis, the Vatican has diligently defended the power structure and traditional sexual teachings of the Church as completely unrelated to the problem. I argue that they are directly related. I see the problem of sexual abuse in the Catholic Church as not only an issue of faith for believers, policy for leaders, justice for victims, and penance for perpetrators but as an issue of systemic social dysfunction that has corrupted Catholicism and other Christian religions over centuries and has created a cycle of toxic sexual shame. This toxicity is so pervasive that sexual abuse of children by priests and nuns is merely one symptom out of many that have yet to be adequately explored by the social sciences.

In the first chapter I offer an overview of the sexual abuse scandal and disclose my own story of abuse as a personal case illustration. It is the case with which I am most familiar, and I have spent many years studying it. In this personal account I decided to use fictitious names not to minimize the burden of responsibility on my perpetrator or those who failed to intervene appropriately but to avoid the potential for distraction from the goal of this book. My story of abuse is only one example of many.

As I have come to know other victims or survivors of abuse by Catholic priests, nuns, and lay employees of the Church, I have recognized that we all portray unique individual differences, as do our perpetrators. However, each of us has certain aspects of our histories that are remarkably common, whether we are male or female, adult or child at the time of the abuse, or abused by a male or a female perpetrator. My story contains many of the same psychological dynamics of sexual abuse and its effects that are experienced by most victims of the Catholic Church sexual abuse crisis who have attempted to work toward a resolution. What is missing from my story that some others have experienced is a sadistic or physically forceful quality to the abuse. The psychological effects of sadistic sexual abuse or rape are often similar to coercive abuse, except that these victims may experience more pronounced visceral reactions to intrusive memories and have greater concerns about personal safety. The tendency toward self-loathing and intense shame that coerced victims experience may occur with less potency for victims of violent abuse, as the extreme lack of physical control in their situations usually allows them to more easily accept that they were not willing participants in their own victimizations.

The four chapters first focus on defining the problem and exploring the contributing factors to the sexual abuse crisis. In Chapter 2, I present a preliminary analysis of the existing data, which suggests that Catholic priests and nuns may be twice to seven times more likely to sexually abuse minors than the general population or other helping professionals, and that both Catholic and Protestant clergy may be more likely to sexually exploit other adults. In addition, distinct characteristics of sexual abuse by priests and nuns offer evidence of a uniquely Catholic problem. My conclusions contradict the assertions of several scholars who have attempted to confront perceived exaggeration of the Catholic Church abuse problem by the media, arguing that sexual abuse by priests (Jenkins, 1996; Plante, 1999, 2002; Rossetti, 2002) and nuns (Markham, 2002) is relatively rare and simply reflects a much bigger problem operating throughout society.

Speculation has emerged about issues such as celibacy, homosexuality, and the hierarchical power structure of the Church as possible causes of the sexual abuse crisis. This has prompted both secular and ecclesiastical debate about how these factors may have contributed to the problem and what can be done about them. Chapter 3 discusses several popular attempts to pinpoint a singular cause, highlighting a common social tendency to assign blame to a scapegoat in order to relieve immediate anxiety and shock in the midst of a crisis. However, none of these popular targets can be causally linked to the sexual abuse of children or other adults by a person in a position of power.

Using a social systems approach, the fourth chapter draws upon parallels between the Church as a human system and a family that has experienced incest. This comparison offers many similarities and provides a framework to apply empirical knowledge from the social sciences about sexually abusive systems. In the next chapter, I review the major psychological theories that attempt to explain sexually abusive behavior. Combined with a systemic perspective and an exploration of Catholic traditions and teachings regarding sexuality, these theories are applied to the unique characteristics of sexual abuse by priests and nuns. I conclude with an argument that systemic sexual shame, as passed down through the beliefs and practices of Catholicism, is the most fundamental factor contributing to a cycle of sexual trauma in the Catholic Church.

The final chapter of the book explores what will be necessary to heal the wounded of the sexual abuse crisis and to achieve resolution in the Church. I assert that it is only through complete, defenseless ownership of the Church's failures that church leaders can begin to move the Church system into recovery from this current crisis and prevent future crises from occurring. Using the analogy of family therapy, options for building functional harmony within and between subsystems of the Church are discussed. Church leaders must be willing to participate in a restructuring of power, support, and communication through a process similar to marital therapy. They must also be willing to work openly with other resources in the global and local communities and to provide responsible "parenting" to all its members, including sexual minorities. The question remains, however, whether there is sufficient motivation and trust among members of the Church to successfully recover from such devastating betrayal.

Chapter 1

The Revelation of Crisis

In 2002, upon learning that bishops knowingly put children at risk and participated in public deception by moving sexually predatory priests from parish to parish, American Catholics were outraged. The bishops had been warned against this practice eighteen years earlier when Reverend Thomas Doyle, one of the Church's top canon lawyers, delivered a report to the U.S. Conference of Catholic Bishops (henceforth referred to as the USCCB) in June 1985. Doyle had joined with a priest psychiatrist, Michael Peterson, and a Catholic civil attorney, Ray Mouton, to create the report that called child sexual abuse by priests "the single most serious and far-reaching problem facing the Church today" (Bruni and Burkett, 2002, p. 163). But bishops failed to realize the devastating implications of the Doyle-Peterson-Mouton report and, in June 2002, were faced with the challenge of addressing the crisis that they had kept under cover for so long. Adding fuel to fire was the discovery that very few of the offending priests known to bishops had ever been reported to civil authorities and that they were instead actively sheltered from criminal charges by their bishops.

Another prominent aspect of the scandal was that it seemed like most of the child victims were male. It was confirmed later that more than 80 percent of allegations reported to dioceses involved young male victims (John Jay College of Criminal Justice, 2004). Most of them were in their early teens at the time of the abuse, and many waited sometimes decades before deciding to come forward. Combining these factors, many Catholics concluded that the bulk of the sexual abuse crisis could be blamed on homosexual priests.

Sexual Abuse and the Culture of Catholicism

doi:10.1300/5633_01

Because these and other issues were at the center of public attention, attempts to understand and address the problem of sexual abuse in the Church were focused primarily on the most salient aspects of the crisis. Under tremendous public scrutiny, the USCCB initially responded to what they assessed to be a policy problem in managing the priesthood, to be dealt with through new policy initiatives and enforcement guidelines as set forth in their *Charter for the Protection of Children and Young People* (2002). The Catholic lay group, Voice of the Faithful, which was initiated soon after the outbreak of scandal in Boston, saw the problem mainly as a failure in leadership at the bishops' level and has since called for greater transparency and accountability in all dioceses. Victim advocacy and support groups, such as the Survivors Network for Those Abused by Priests (SNAP) and The Linkup, have demanded greater attention to the tremendous harm suffered by individual survivors and have insisted that all alleged abusers be publicly identified and stripped of any clerical status, which might assist them in abusing again.

Meanwhile, certain political groups within the Church have seized the opportunity to promote their own agendas and point to what they see as the primary sources of the problem, including an all-male clergy, mandatory celibacy, and the acceptance of gay men into the priesthood. In state legislatures, advocates for victims have tested the boundaries of the First Amendment's separation of church and state by seeking to overturn statutes of limitation on criminal and civil suits against the Church and adding clergy to state laws, mandating them to report knowledge of child abuse to the police.

While these approaches have attempted to address the most obvious concerns, none of them penetrate the underlying questions as to why these spiritual leaders were drawn to sexually exploiting children in the first place and how others could have allowed such abuses to go on for so long. In addition, none of these approaches considers abuses perpetrated by women religious or lay ministers. A number of Catholic scholars and journalists have offered more complex analyses of the underlying factors they believe contributed to the sexual abuse crisis. Each of them offers insights based on years of professional experience working with priests or investigating clerical sexual abuse.

Journalist-author Jason Berry (Berry, 1992; Berry and Renner, 2004), who initially exposed the first wave of cases in the 1980s, has detailed a description of the self-serving culture of clerical elitism in the Catholic Church, which allows perpetrator priests to offend repeatedly while maintaining privileged and protected status in the fold. Catholic psychologists, some of them priests or former priests, have reflected on their own observations of sexual exploitation from within the clerical culture. A.W. Richard Sipe (1995, 2003) describes what he thinks led to the current crisis as the fallacy of a celibate priesthood, a seminary structure that protects or postpones adolescence, and a dangerous distortion of sex and power within the clerical culture. Similarly, Eugene Kennedy (2001) claims that the Catholic Church's failure to understand and appreciate the complexities of human sexuality has produced some priests who are so sexually "wounded" that they prey upon the weakest in their flocks for temporary relief from their own pain. Stephen Rossetti (2002) clarifies his point that, while homosexuality may be a factor in the sexual abuse crisis, the proclivity of some priests to abuse boys has more to do with psychosexual immaturity. Finally, Donald Cozzens (2002) explains how church leaders have become dependent on collective denial to manage their overwhelming feelings of anxiety related to post-modern sexual issues. Consequently, they have clung to the comfort of silence in the face of mounting problems in the Church, including sexual abuse.

These theoretical analyses offer insight into a complex dysfunctional system that warrants further investigation. However, like other approaches to the problem of sexual abuse in the Church, their analyses are limited by considering only sexual abuse perpetrated by priests. Perhaps their greatest challenges are that they are based primarily on anecdotal evidence and that they fail to offer a valid comparative context in which to weigh their arguments. What remains most lacking in any etiological discussion of the Catholic sexual abuse problem are valid, empirical data and analytical research that compare sexual abuse perpetrated by Catholic priests, deacons, and religious men and women to sexual offenses by members of other professional groups and by men and women in the general population. As John Allan Loftus (1999, p. 15), one of the leading researchers on clergy sexual misconduct, put it, "Despite many laudable attempts to pursue better sexual and celibate education for clergy and seminarians, to put in place preventive care programs, to design relapse prevention systems for those who had transgressed, we are still largely aiming our guns in the dark." Until recently, the available data on the prevalence and characteristics of abuse in the Church was very limited. Now, we have descriptive statistics on reports of child sexual abuse committed by priests and deacons, but there are still sizeable gaps of information on adult sexual exploitation and sexual abuse perpetrated by women religious (nuns), religious brothers, and lay ministers.

A PERSONAL CASE STUDY

In August 1977, I stepped into my seventh-grade classroom and met my homeroom teacher, Sr. Ann. She was new to our rural Louisiana Catholic School and the first nun I had ever seen dressed in regular street clothes. She was young and energetic. At first I tested her, as I did with all of my teachers, to see if she could be challenging enough to hold my attention. Sr. Ann quickly won my respect, always having a sharp response to even my most provocative questions.

One afternoon, a few months into the first semester, Sr. Ann slipped an envelope on my desk just before the final bell rang to go home. My heart pounded when I opened a card that read, "You Are Special." Inside was a message saying that although our relationship was "stormy at times," I was very special to her "as a student and a friend." I was both flattered and afraid.

Soon afterward, I approached her to inquire about the process of becoming a nun. She explained to me that it was not for everyone; "you have to have a calling." She described this as a deep yearning to serve God in a way that was different from what most people experience. She said that taking vows of poverty, chastity, and obedience was like marrying God and her religious community instead of a husband. I was intrigued by the idea of an alternative role in life than what my mother had modeled for me.

I was a naive and high-spirited girl, the youngest of six daughters with a ten-year age span. My sisters often teased me because I was such a tomboy and a "late bloomer." By the time I was twelve, my parents were eager to find time away from the family to rekindle a social life. My father had worked long hours for many years to build a business to provide for the family, and my mother had often been overwhelmed with the responsibilities of caring for so many children who were so close in age. When Sr. Ann took a special interest in me, my parents welcomed the extra attention she was willing to offer.

SR. MOTHER MOLESTER

We began sitting next to each other in the lunchroom, talking during recesses and after school. We debated issues in politics, theology, psychology, and social justice. She shared stories with me of her teenage years in New Orleans before she entered the convent—about the guy she dated and decided not to marry, about going to Beatles concerts and Mardi Gras parades, and about growing up in an urban, working-class family. She read her poetry to me, and we analyzed our dreams together. All the while, Sr. Ann assured me that I was very mature for my age—"I was special." I soaked up the attention and began to think of her as a mother figure. Eventually, she invited me to address her simply as "Ann."

In the summer after seventh grade, Sr. Ann left to attend classes in Texas. The separation was difficult but we kept in touch with letters and occasional phone calls. In the eighth grade, she was my religion teacher. Our relationship continued to assume a more romantic quality with nightly phone calls, letter and poetry writing, and simple gifts like candles and rosaries. When rumors of favoritism started circulating among my classmates, Sr. Ann and I began meeting at the convent after school and over weekends instead of during school hours. Our intellectual debates turned into playful wrestling on the swing out back or upstairs in her room. Sometimes when she pinned me down she would kiss me on the mouth. Eventually she initiated "French kissing," which at first seemed very odd to me, but I did not question it—I assumed it was "mature."

My parents started allowing Sr. Ann to stay with me on weekends if they were out of town and my older sisters were unavailable. They would let me go with her on overnight trips to visit her family or to attend events at her congregation's motherhouse. During these overnight stays Sr. Ann would sleep with me, each time initiating more progressive sexual contact. It would usually start with her requesting that I rub her back or stomach. Then she would direct my hands elsewhere or begin touching me. When I would pull away from her, she would cry. In guilt, I would reach out to comfort her, and again the sexual contact would start. This time I would go along with it to appease her. The sexual contact progressed from kissing to fondling to genital stimulation. My body responded in ways that were foreign to me, but I was too scared to ask questions. The next day there would be no mention of what had happened.

As Sr. Ann and I spent more time together, people began to notice that our friendship was unusual. My parents, their friends, and other teachers assumed that she was mentoring me for religious life. In my Cajun culture, it was considered a blessing to have a child with a religious vocation. I had always been perceived as the "holy one" in the family; my mother often asked me to pray for her intentions because she thought I had "more pull with God." My older sisters, however, thought my relationship with this nun was strange, and they teased me about "acting like Sr. Ann was my boyfriend."

When Sr. Ann and I discussed the nature of our relationship, it was always in a spiritual context. She believed that our connection was a very personal gift from God and should be cherished and celebrated. This explanation seemed somehow to justify the secrecy of the relationship, since others would not be capable of understanding its sacredness. I took comfort in Sr. Ann's affection, eager to believe that I could be so uniquely blessed.

Over the summer of 1979, Sr. Ann again had to leave for classes. We spent as much time together as we could until the day she left, and then wrote letters almost daily. When she returned to teach at the middle school, I was entering high school at a different location. At the age of fourteen, I had become emotionally isolated from my peers, yet I was still respected as a high achiever and a teacher's pet. I had the convenience of hiding behind the reputation that my older sisters had established: that we were a family of outgoing leaders who would always enjoy popularity in our school. But I felt different. When my sisters and other girls would talk about dating and kissing boys, the reality of my experience became more apparent to me. I recognized that what had evolved between Sr. Ann and me was not normal.

The naive fantasy I once had—that Sr. Ann and I would spend the rest of our lives together—gave way to the shameful realization that I had been participating in a homosexual affair with a woman who had already vowed herself to God. I no longer felt blessed. I felt sinful, like a pervert and an adulteress.

In September 1979, in the beginning of my first year of high school, one of my older sisters committed suicide at the age of seventeen. As rumors stirred that my sister may have been pregnant, I felt even more isolated and ashamed. It was never determined why my sister killed herself, only that she was not pregnant at the time and she did not leave a note. While my parents became consumed with grief, I felt more and more alone. The secrecy and shame of my relationship with Sr. Ann had become a tremendous burden to me, but after my sister's suicide I was so vulnerable and emotionally isolated that I clung to our friendship more than ever.

Several months later, though, some of the other nuns began to express discomfort with my frequent presence at the convent and the amount of time Sr. Ann was spending with me in her room. At one point, we discussed the "physical aspect" of our relationship as wrong and discrediting to its greater sanctity. Yet, the sexual contact continued. Sr. Ann believed that we were both at fault for failing to resist sexual temptation. I became overwhelmed by this and eventually turned to another nun for help. But my language about the relationship, shrouded in a spiritual context, was so vague and awkward that she did not understand what I needed from her. I was too scared and embarrassed to talk about what was happening between Sr. Ann and me in direct sexual terms. The nun I turned to was untrained or too naïve to interpret my awkwardness.

In February 1980, I turned fifteen and got my driver's license and a hand-me-down car to call my own. With increased scrutiny at the convent, we limited our time together there to when the other nuns were out of town. One Saturday that spring, I got home after spending the night at the convent to find my mother very upset. She said that Sr. Ann's Provincial Director, Sr. Juanita, had just called her from the congregation's motherhouse. She had received a report about a neighbor of the convent witnessing Sr. Ann and me kissing in a car. Sr. Juanita and my mother had agreed to confront us separately, and I was to call Sr. Juanita later that afternoon. I was terrified of what might happen next.

My mother asked about the nature of the kissing, which I affirmed was open-mouth and prolonged. I could not speak through my sobbing to offer more information than that. My mother was furious, referring to Sr. Ann as a demon who had contaminated me. I was forbidden to have contact with Sr. Ann ever again or to share with anyone else what had happened to me. I assumed that my mother understood the full nature of the relationship Sr. Ann had created.

When I called Sr. Juanita that afternoon, she began by expressing concern for me. Then she explained that after confronting Sr. Ann, she determined that Sr. Ann would be immediately relocated from my hometown to the motherhouse and placed in psychiatric care. I assumed Sr. Ann told her everything. Sr. Juanita went on to say that she knew it would be difficult for me to experience the loss of this friendship but that it needed to end because "the relationship was wrong."

I did not hear anything from Sr. Ann for several weeks, until she called me one night to say that she was alright. She was seeing a psychiatrist and living at the motherhouse. She revealed that she would be teaching adult education in a church parish but that Sr. Juanita had restricted her from working with children and adolescents. From then on, Sr. Ann and I would occasionally sneak phone calls or letters to each other, but I eventually quit seeking contact. I came to resent her emotional dependence on me and felt that she had manipulated me. After getting caught once by my mother in a phone call from Sr. Ann, I felt conflicted about my alliances. I was in a no-win situation: either I betrayed Sr. Ann by cutting her off, or I betrayed my mother by maintaining contact with her. I retreated from both.

THE SECRET

My mother told no one of the abuse, not even my father. I believe now that her intention was to protect me from town gossip, but for me it only drove the shame deeper. She never asked about the details of our physical contact. She knew about the kissing and that was enough for her. Once, she took me to see a psychiatrist, but I resisted, thinking she only wanted to "fix" me so I would not turn out to be a lesbian. The psychiatrist gave me a clean bill of health based on my level of academic and extracurricular achievement. But my mother continued to pressure me to "act normal," wear makeup, and date boys. She strongly discouraged me from associating with other nuns or from considering a religious vocation. As she continued to grieve my sister's suicide, I often felt her turning to me for reassurance that she had been a good mother. My relationship with her was strained throughout my high school years, though on the surface I did my best to please her. I became heavily involved in after-school activities and academic clubs to avoid being at home alone with her.

While I functioned well as a very active student, I continued to feel ashamed and dishonest with my peers. I thought that if they ever found out about my past, they would reject and despise me. I struggled with guilt in my spiritual life as well, experiencing only partial relief after confessing my "sins" of homosexual activity and adultery against God to our parish priest at the age of sixteen. While he expressed concern for me and disagreed that I was guilty of adultery in this situation, he did give me absolution for my "sexual sins." He never once qualified my experience as sexual abuse, and he never made a report on my behalf to anyone who could help me or my family to cope with this trauma. While I felt some relief from my confession, I continued to blame myself for what happened. I felt forgiven by God, but not by my mother.

In 1983, I graduated from high school and left home to attend college at Loyola University in New Orleans. My major was psychology with a minor in religious studies. Despite my negative experiences and my mother's discouragement, I still wondered if I had "a calling" to religious life. I developed relationships with vocation directors of several different religious congregations, but I still felt most drawn to the group of women who had taught me throughout my childhood. The problem, of course, was that I knew I would have to address my past if I were to consider entering the same congregation as Sr. Ann. I knew that I would need Sr. Juanita's approval as the Provincial Director before I could explore it any further.

I got in touch with Sr. Ann, first, to discuss my intentions and to seek closure with her. While she seemed pleased to be in contact with me again, catching me up on her recent years, she was very resistant to the idea of my affiliating with her congregation. She anxiously explained that if the other sisters in her community were to find out about our past relationship, they might misconstrue it, creating negative consequences for both of us. We agreed to keep the physical details of our relationship in the past and try to move on with our lives.

It was the spring of 1984 when I contacted Sr. Juanita to express my interest in learning more about the order and possibly becoming an affiliate. She arranged for a special meeting to discuss the implications with her and the congregation's formation director, Sr. Claire. At this meeting, we discussed my "relationship with Sr. Ann," the resulting strain in my relationship with my mother, and the suicide of my sister. They felt that because of these events, I should not become an affiliate of their congregation until I had lived at least another year "being a normal college student." They also recommended that I seek spiritual direction, preferably from a man.

I left the meeting feeling crushed, hopeless, and unwanted. Never in our discussion did they clarify that what had happened between Sr. Ann and me was not my fault. Nor did they acknowledge that this "relationship" between a twenty-six-year-old nun and her pubescent student was sexual abuse, for which they shared some responsibility for failing to protect me, a child in the care of their organization. Instead, Sr. Juanita and Sr. Claire, like me, referred to my "relationship with Sr. Ann" by using only vague language and obtuse terms.

I did seek spiritual direction soon afterward and participated actively in campus ministry. But in the year that followed, my relationships with peers became my primary focus, and I gave up exploring religious life. I dated a few young men during this time but never felt emotionally connected to them and struggled with intrusive memories of the abuse. Ultimately, I did fall in love for the first time, which was not only exciting for me but also terrifying. My first serious romantic interest as an adult was directed toward another student I had befriended through campus ministry activities, another victim of childhood sexual abuse by a female teacher, someone I felt could truly understand me. She was also a young woman. I wrestled endlessly with what this might mean for my faith and my sexual identity, but most of all I questioned how it might be related to my experience with Sr. Ann. The result was that I blamed myself even more for what had happened back then. In considering this new relationship, I was also terrified of the consequences it might have on my fragile relationship with my mother. Ultimately, with the exception of a few close friends, my partner and I resorted to living in secrecy.

ERUPTION OF SHAME

Then, in December 1985, my mother died of heart failure after undergoing a routine angioplasty. All of the pain and shame from the past came surging to the surface again. I felt guilty for having caused my mother such grief because of my involvement with Sr. Ann. I wondered if this had contributed to her early death at the age of fifty-two years. I felt I was a huge disappointment to her, and now I had no way of resolving it with her. I became very depressed, angry, and withdrawn, pulling away especially from my partner.

My father became the focus of the family after my mother's death. He struggled to adjust to life without her, but eventually fell into depression as well. Despite our efforts to help him, and the trust we placed in his psychiatric care, my father killed himself in January 1987, just over a year after my mother's death. Again, I felt responsible. Yet, no one in the family knew what I was feeling. It had all been kept secret.

The familiar feelings of isolation and shame came back with a vengeance. My partner could no longer tolerate my despair, and left me for another woman one month after my father's suicide. I not only felt betrayed by her but abandoned by God. I quickly spiraled further into severe depression. A campus minister referred me to the student health center for counseling, and I was placed on antidepressants. But the source of my shame was never addressed. I began using marijuana and alcohol to try to mask my feelings of worthlessness, but they only made things worse. I managed to graduate in August 1987, based on a history of high academic performance in previous years, but the accomplishment meant nothing to me without someone there to be proud of me.

Shortly after finishing classes, I attempted suicide with pills, only to be discovered by a roommate. This resulted in a brief hospital stay and another trial of counseling and antidepressants. Six months later, I tried to hang myself but failed once again. The same campus minister who had intervened once before referred me, this time, to a social worker off campus for more in-depth psychotherapy. After several sessions, I finally disclosed to her the source of tension between my mother and me as the "relationship with Sr. Ann." Now, nearly a decade later, this therapist was the first person to identify that Sr. Ann had sexually abused me. The therapist explained that my feelings of shame were part of a syndrome experienced by many victims of sexual abuse. But this new definition brought no relief. I just became more ashamed for having allowed myself to be victimized.

On June 4, 1988, I tried again to kill myself, this time with near fatality. Once again, my roommates intercepted and rushed me to the hospital. When my physical condition stabilized, I was placed in an in-patient psychiatric facility near my hometown, where I could be closer to my sisters for additional support. I was discharged after about a week and started intensive outpatient treatment while living with my oldest sister and her family. I participated in individual, family, and group psychotherapy as well as therapeutic massage for seven months there before I was considered safe enough to leave for graduate school and continue my treatment there.

RECOVERY

For many years, while I explored educational, relationship, and career pursuits, I continued to rely on individual and group therapy to help me fight my inner struggles with self-defeating thoughts, fears of intimacy, and mistrust of others. As I gained emotional strength and insight into how my childhood experiences affected me, I felt compelled to help others who might have experienced similar trauma or neglect. I changed my career focus from animal behavior research to clinical social work and obtained an MSW degree in December 1990. I began working with children and families in crisis, victims and perpetrators of abuse, and I taught classes in sexual abuse prevention.

Through the years, I continued to grow and develop, professionally and personally. Each relationship brought unique challenges, which I learned to accept as opportunities for self-reflection and healing. I am now happily out as a lesbian, in a loving, committed relationship, and enjoy a very close and supportive network of family and friends. I look back on those years of suicidal depression and feel blessed to have made it through them alive.

In the spring of 2002, when the issue of sexual abuse by Catholic priests was brought into the public spotlight, I was preoccupied with moving and career transitions for both my partner and me. Amidst the tasks of getting resettled, it was easy for me to escape the media reports of the Boston scandal. Friends were surprised when they inquired about my views on the topic and I responded by minimizing the story's relevance to me. Eventually, though, the news coverage became so overwhelming that avoiding it was impossible. One morning, I found myself trembling in front of the television, hearing of yet another allegation and the attempted murder of an alleged priest perpetrator by his victim. Later that day, a nun dressed in habit, dining at the same restaurant where I was having lunch, caught my eye. Seemingly without reason, a sense of anger and disgust, which I had not felt in a long time, welled up inside me. I could not finish my lunch, and I could no longer ignore the scandal's effect on me. It was with reluctance then, that I realized I still had work to do in my own recovery.

Although I had personally confronted Sr. Ann about the abuse as part of my therapy in 1988, I had never reported her to civil authorities or confronted Sr. Juanita and the rest of her congregational leaders for failing to take responsibility for my welfare. I was in denial about how my experience of abuse from Sr. Ann also had dangerous implications for the rest of society. I wanted to believe that I was the only victim. I had trusted that Sr. Juanita and the major superiors who followed her would monitor Sr. Ann to make sure she never abused again. I did not want to think about it any more. I wanted to leave it in the past.

As the exposure of sexual abuse in the Church continued to grow, one thing in particular became more apparent to me. No one was talking about abuse by nuns. Surely Sr. Ann was not the only nun who had ever sexually abused a student or child in her care. So why were not their victims speaking up? Eventually, I had to ask myself the same question. I began to feel like a hypocrite for remaining silent as a social worker. On the other hand, I could not imagine going through the process of reliving such painful memories in order to "go public" with my story.

With more reflection on my hesitation, I realized that there was still a part of me that wanted to protect Sr. Ann from public scrutiny. There was a part of me that wanted to hold on to my childish image of her as a nurturing mother figure. I wanted to believe that she was different from those perpetrators exposed in the media because she said she loved me. But through my own work in therapy and in my experience as a therapist, I have learned that this struggle is a common effect of childhood sexual abuse, particularly in cases of parental incest. I recognized my naivete in believing that I was Sr. Ann's only victim, or that she represented an enigma among women religious. As difficult as it was to accept, I knew that I would have to face the truth of my own experience before I could expect others to understand the full scope of this crisis. With this realization, keeping my silence was no longer an option.

CONFRONTATION

My first step was to consult my partner, friends, family, and former therapists, who were all very encouraging. Next, I sought out legal advice from a well-known attorney, Anthony Fontana, who had successfully represented dozens of victims of clergy sexual abuse in the 1980s and 1990s. But since the abuse had occurred more than 20 years earlier, my legal options were limited. Although he was willing to advocate on my behalf, I felt a need to stay in control. I felt that in order to achieve the maximum benefits of reclaiming my personal power, I needed to confront on my own the system that had failed me. Mr. Fontana did help me to clarify my goals and suggested that I write a statement of what had happened to me and what I was seeking now.

My main objective became very clear. I wanted to alert church officials and the general public as soon as possible that nuns needed to be included in the investigations and policy considerations that were already underway within the Church. I thought that using the media to tell my story would be the quickest means to reach that goal. If the Church ignored my warning, at least the public would be made aware that nuns, as with all other trusted caregivers of children, are capable of abusing the power we give them. I hoped to reach other victims as well, perhaps to offer them some relief in knowing they are not alone.

On a deeper level, I wished to restore my faith in the community of women who had first instilled in me a passion for justice. I hoped that they would respond to me differently from how the bishops had responded to victims of priests. I wanted them to prove to me that there is still a place where healing and reconciliation are possible for those who have been hurt by the Catholic Church. Because I could no longer deny the betrayal I experienced by Sr. Ann, I was attempting to salvage any remaining trust I could in the women who had taught me virtue as a child, the women I had once held up as my role models.

On May 31, 2002, less than a week before the U.S. Conference of Catholic Bishops met in Dallas to create new policies on the issue, I read in the newspaper that the local Archdiocese had established a hotline, staffed by lay professionals, to receive reports of abuse by clergy. Three days later, I called, still hesitant to trust the process without legal representation. I was told that this new reporting process had only been established to hear reports of abuse at the hands of priests and deacons. To report abuse by a nun, I was told to call the Vicar of Women Religious, Sr. Stephanie. I recognized her full name as a former superior and personal friend of Sr. Ann's from the same congregation of nuns. I was shocked and angered that the very person I was now supposed to trust and report to was someone who had previously failed to protect me.

When I called her, I disclosed my story with caution to keep my identity and the identity of my abuser concealed. She expressed sincere sympathy. Then she explained that the prescribed procedure was to contact the current director of my abuser's congregation to make a report. The congregation's leadership would then investigate my allegations. I was surprised at how understanding and supportive she was as I vented my anger about how biased this system of internal investigation seemed to be. And, when I eventually revealed that my abuser was a member of her own congregation, she was emotionally shaken and genuine with me in acknowledging her limitations to being objective. This candor allowed me to trust her and to question my longstanding assumption that Sr. Ann's superiors all knew of the abuse after the original report was made in 1980.

I approached the call to the current congregational director, also a nun whose name I recognized, with greater skepticism. She was the same woman, Sr. Claire, who had been the formation director present in the meeting with Sr. Juanita and me in 1984. I felt certain that she had known the full extent of my "relationship with Sr. Ann" since the time of that meeting. I assumed that Sr. Juanita had briefed her on the details of the abuse and that she had joined her congregation's leadership in maintaining the secret. I thought that calling her now would not be a report of new allegations but a dreaded reminder of what she hoped would remain in the past. I thought it would simply be a matter of resurrecting the documentation from 1980.

Despite my suspicions of Sr. Claire, she reacted with genuine shock when I made my report. She said she had no reason to doubt my story, but denied remembering me or ever knowing of the sexual abuse before my call. She also told me that Sr. Juanita had died many years ago. I told her I felt certain that there would be something about the sexual abuse in Sr. Ann's file, because that was why she was removed from my hometown so abruptly and placed in psychiatric care in 1980. She promised to check the file that evening and get back to me the next day before leaving the country for a month.

Sr. Claire did call as she had promised and said that she had postponed her departure in order to launch a major investigation into my allegations. She said that she had already alerted their attorney, the general administrative council, all previous superiors, and Sr. Ann.

Suddenly I panicked. The reality of Sr. Ann's existence in the present tense tore through the mental barriers I had established over the years to keep her safely in the past. Then Sr. Claire asked me to think about whether I wanted to use an attorney to represent me in communicating with their attorney or if I wanted to handle this directly with her. I was very confused, anxious, and guarded for the following weeks, but I was determined to use direct communication and/or professional mediation as a process of healing instead of pursuing a legal battle of win or lose.

On June 18, 2002, I submitted a letter to Sr. Claire, requesting her cooperation in addressing the need for prevention of sexual abuse by Catholic religious, rather than focusing solely on punishment for abusers. I invited her to join me in approaching the media with this case so that we might demonstrate a model for healing, facing our wounds side by side. I requested that her congregation become an advocate for psychological and sociological research into the factors that contribute to sexual abuse by women religious. I also wanted assurance that Sr. Ann had been removed from public ministry with children and adolescents, that she was being closely monitored, and that an effort was made to locate other potential victims. Finally, I wanted the congregation to take some responsibility for my welfare and to be accountable for how they had handled the original report of misconduct in 1980. For this, I requested compensation for my past mental health expenses and full disclosure of what action was taken when Sr. Juanita first learned about the "relationship" Sr. Ann was having with her twelve- to fifteen-year-old student.

Sr. Claire delayed a response to my specific requests for several weeks while an internal investigation was being conducted and while she was out of the country. In the meantime, I launched into my own search for other survivors and information on sexual abuse by nuns, women, Catholic clergy, other helping professionals, and other religious leaders. I was desperate to know if there were others like me out there and if there was any published research on the issue. I was eager to make sense of my own experience by combing through professional literature and media stories of abuse while searching for themes and patterns that would tie our experiences together into a more meaningful theory that could explain the underlying causes of sexual abuse in the Church.

The Internet was an invaluable resource to connect with other survivors. I joined an online support group for women abused by nuns either in childhood or as young novices in religious communities. The group was initiated by Ashley Hill, a survivor and author of the first book to address the issue, *Habits of Sin: An Expose of Nuns Who Sexually Abuse Children and Each Other* (1995). Reading the stories of other women and knowing that many of them were in their fifties and sixties before they revealed their abuse solidified my conviction to speak out publicly. If I reached only one other victim, it would be worth the risk of harassment from nonbelievers and sensation seekers. I became very close to my Internet friends, and their support got me through many difficult times.

Finding a news source that was willing to do a story on sexual abuse by nuns became my next challenge. I presented my story to the *Boston Globe* through a social acquaintance of mine who had done some freelance work for them. I was told that her editor passed it on to the Spotlight Team and that I should expect to hear from them directly. As it turned out, I never heard from them and I assumed my story got lost in the shuffle of the Boston scandal. I was beginning to get discouraged by the lack of response from other attempts when I got a call from Anthony Fontana, the attorney whom I had first consulted. He said a local reporter had contacted him, seeking stories on female victims of clergy abuse, but he persuaded him to explore abuse by female religious perpetrators instead. I jumped on the opportunity to tell my story. This reporter, Louis Rom, wrote the first comprehensive articles on the topic, including interviews with several victims and experts in treating religious sexual offenders. The story was published in two local weekly newspapers in August 2002, and again in *National Catholic Reporter* in November (Rom, 2002a, 2002b, 2002c). However, the issue of sexual abuse by women religious was slow to get national attention, and was downplayed as an extremely rare phenomenon that was already being properly addressed by congregational leaders (Donovan, 2002). It became obvious to me that not only the Church but also the general public was resistant to conceiving of nuns as possible child molesters.

Though I hoped that Sr. Claire would offer her own perspective as a religious leader for Rom to include in his articles, at the time Sr. Claire was still out of the country and reluctant to trust a reporter from the public media. She responded to his e-mails with only minimal acknowledgment that I had been in touch with her. She maintained that any specific information on the investigation of my allegations was confidential. Sr. Claire did, however, confirm for him that there had been an allegation of an "inappropriate relationship" in 1980 and that the sister in question had been removed from ministry at that time.

When Sr. Claire returned to the city, she requested an opportunity to offer a "pastoral response" to me while their investigation was still underway. She arranged for a meeting with her, her assistant, and a support person of my choice, but refused to include a therapeutic mediator, based on advice from her lawyer. Though I would have preferred a meeting in a neutral location with an objective professional to facilitate, Sr. Claire persuaded me to meet with her first before deciding whether mediation was necessary. At this meeting, in a guest home across the street from their convent and administrative offices, she and her assistant welcomed my partner and me and expressed their own sorrow as I shared the emotional turmoil I had been through. Again, Sr. Claire made it clear that she believed me.

When I asked why the investigation was taking more than four weeks at that point, they revealed that there had been no record of the original report made in 1980 and that my allegations were being investigated as a new complaint. Sr. Claire also reported that Sr. Ann was denying any sexual contact between us and, with no direct witnesses, they could only conclude with certainty that the relationship was "emotionally inappropriate" and damaging to me. Apparently, Sr. Ann had never confessed the sexual abuse to Sr. Juanita on that day when we were both confronted. According to Sr. Ann's record, she was placed in psychiatric care not for sexually abusing me but for depression. I suddenly felt betrayed all over again. How could I have been so gullible to believe Sr. Ann when she said she had told her superiors "all about us?" I had assumed that Sr. Juanita had acted responsibly when Sr. Ann told me that she would only be allowed to work with adults from then on. I trusted that her community leaders, the nuns I looked up to even after the abuse, were monitoring Sr. Ann to make sure she never abused again. My whole body ached as I realized that my longstanding notions of righteousness were nothing more than illusions.

I met with Sr. Claire four more times over the next several months. It became very important to me that she fulfill the role of a gentle, compassionate, and fair leader, despite my reluctance to trust her. I wanted to know how she was feeling through this process as well. I needed to know that she was a real person, responding to me with as much honesty and trust as was required of me to share myself with her. At that point in time, Sr. Claire represented the ultimate Mother and my last hope to restore faith in the moral standard of the Church. How she responded to me, Sr. Ann, and the rest of her community would determine the path of my healing.

Sr. Claire did offer me her own feelings, her compassion, and acceptance. She treated me with respect while holding fast to her responsibilities to her community sisters, including Sr. Ann. She met as many of my requests as I believe she could, including educational programs on sexual abuse for all community personnel, revision of their sexual abuse policies, an online statement about the congregation's response to the sexual abuse crisis, and full, uncontested compensation for my past mental health expenses. Unfortunately, Sr. Claire stopped short of issuing an official conclusion regarding my allegation of sexual abuse, despite her public acknowledgement that the relationship involved "inappropriate sexual behavior" in one news report after our initial meeting (Pawlaczyk, 2002, p. 1A). The consequences of emotionally abusive behavior according to their policies were the same as for sexual abuse, so Sr. Claire did not press their investigation further.

While I now trust Sr. Claire to make sure that Sr. Ann will never have opportunity within the Church to abuse children again, I have no way of knowing whether Sr. Ann will leave her community and continue to live and work independently of the Church without supervision. Her whereabouts are confidential, as well as her ministry status. These restrictions in information, combined with an inconclusive verdict regarding the sexual abuse, keep me from achieving resolution, and I continue to feel powerless in relation to my abuser. While I understand that Sr. Ann is entitled to her privacy as she has not been convicted of a crime in a court of law, it feels very different to me as a victim. My feelings on this issue vacillate between feeling betrayed by both the Church and the state and feeling ashamed of myself for having failed to report the abuse within the statute of limitations. I have never wanted Sr. Ann to go to jail, but I do want her and the public to be spared the experience of another lapse in her judgment.

It is this sense of powerlessness that has driven me to search for a deeper understanding of how this could happen to me and what contributed to Sr. Ann becoming a sexual predator. How is it that both my mother and Sr. Juanita thought it would be best to minimize the abuse as opposed to exploring it further and reporting it to the police? What role did sexual orientation and homophobia play in how my abuse occurred and how it was handled? Would Sr. Ann have been less inclined to abuse me if she had not attempted to live a life of celibacy? What does my story have in common with other stories of abuse by nuns and priests? What is different about my story that may shed new light on this crisis in the Church?

Knowledge offers hope and power. If these questions can be answered, then perhaps something can be done to minimize sexual abuse by religious ministers in the future. Perhaps with a greater understanding of underlying factors, church leaders can work more effectively to prevent their dedicated ministers from becoming sexual predators. Perhaps the faithful will be better prepared to circumvent potentially harmful relationships. And when abuse does occur, perhaps the traumatic effects can be lessened by immediate healing support.

Through my attempts to answer my own questions with the mindset of an experienced clinician and social scientist, I have gained insight that I hope will be helpful to others seeking a deeper understanding of the sexual abuse crisis. This book was written with a broad audience in mind: diocesan, religious, and lay leaders of the Catholic Church; mental health, legal, and civil service professionals who work with Catholic clients or constituents; social science researchers who may wish to pursue further study in this area; faithful lay and religious members of the Church; and those who have been abused by priests, nuns, brothers, or anyone in a position of trust and authority acting in the name of God.

Chapter 2

Taking a Closer Look: Prevalence and Characteristics of Sexual Abuse in the Catholic Church

In February 2004, results were released from a study commissioned by the U.S. Conference of Catholic Bishops (USCCB)-appointed National Review Board for the Protection of Children and Youth (henceforth referred to as the National Review Board or NRB) and conducted by the John Jay College of Criminal Justice in New York. Surveys were sent to all dioceses and religious orders of men in the United States in order to collect data on the number of allegations and the number from 1950 to 2002 of priests and deacons accused of sexually abusing minors. The results provide us with the best data available on the extent of child sexual abuse perpetrated by priests and deacons, despite some concerns about its self-report design and inconsistencies in procedures between dioceses. Nonetheless, this study offers a starting place to assess how Catholic priests and religious compare with clergy from other denominations, with professionals in other service-related fields, and with men and women in the general population.

Although published research on similar professional groups is sparse, and prevalence estimates for the general population have not been previously examined, the available data offer enough to conduct a preliminary comparative review. This chapter explores differences and similarities in the prevalence and characteristics of child sexual abuse and adult sexual exploitation/assault perpetrated by Roman Catholic priests, nuns, other Christian clergy, mental health professionals, educators, and the general population of men and women in

Sexual Abuse and the Culture of Catholicism

doi:10.1300/5633_02

the Unites States. This preliminary review suggests that Catholic priests and nuns may have a greater likelihood of sexually abusing minors than other helping professionals or men and women in general. In addition, characteristics of sexual abuse by priests and nuns more closely resemble patterns of incest than compulsive pedophilia or other types of sexual offending.

PREVALENCE

Estimating the percentage of any population that has ever sexually violated a child or vulnerable adult is a very difficult task. There are two different sources of information: perpetrators and victims. Gathering information from either source is limited by the willingness of individuals to disclose their experiences with an issue that is highly personal, emotionally charged, and, in the case of perpetrators, self-incriminating. Typically, information from perpetrators is generated by anonymous surveys of the population being studied or data from clinical facilities that serve the population.

In addition to these methods, information from victims can also come in the form of reports of abuses to authorities. It is generally believed that sexual violations are under-reported in all populations because of the shame and secrecy instilled in victims as a result of the abuse. Therefore, data generated from reports of abuse to authorities are usually much less than data collected from anonymous surveys of perpetrator populations, although both forms of data are assumed to result in underestimates of actual prevalence. For child sexual abuse, studies indicate that only about half of victims ever disclose the abuse (Putnam, 2003). Less than a third of all rapes and sexual assaults against victims of age twelve years and older are ever reported to police (U.S. Census Bureau, 2003, No. 315). Of the cases that are reported to and investigated by civil or corporate authorities, only a third of alleged perpetrators ever admit to abuse upon evaluation (Abel and Harlow, 2001).

After prolific news coverage of hundreds of cases of abuse by priests, many Americans started to question whether sexual abuse is more common in the Catholic Church than in other areas of society. Experts have been repeatedly quoted by journalists, explaining the limits of research in this area (Donn and Ritter, 2002; Moller, 2003; Rodgers, 2004). Until this scandal in the Catholic Church, social science research had primarily focused on the rates of *victimization* rather than *perpetration* of child sexual abuse in various populations. This gives us information on how many people have been abused, but we know very little about the number of people who have perpetrated the offenses. The prevalence of sexual abuse perpetration in the general population has never been directly studied.

This gap in professional knowledge on perpetration rates did not stop some Catholic officials from trying to defend the Church from what they believed was a disproportionate and unfair emphasis in the media on abuses by priests. Cardinal Joseph Ratzinger, who has since become Pope Benedict XVI, was quoted in *National Catholic Reporter* as claiming, "The percentage of these offenses among priests is not higher than in other categories, and perhaps it is even lower" (Donovan, 2003, p. 2). Archbishop Julian Herranz, president of the Pontifical Council for the Interpretation of Legislative Texts, took this hyperbolic minimization one step further by proclaiming as facts figures for which he could offer no evidence to support: "Pedophilia is only minimally identified with the Church, touching scarcely one percent of priests. Meanwhile, for other categories of persons, the percentages are much higher" (Allen, 2003b, p. 9).

Even psychology researcher and author Thomas Plante (2002) felt moved to defend the Church by referring to estimates of priestly abuse as lower than in the general adult male population, which he estimated, without any clarification of his source or methods, as close to 8 percent.

An "antidefamation" group, called the Catholic League for Religious and Civil Rights, posted a special report on its Web site in February 2004, just before the findings of the John Jay College study were released, in an effort to keep public discussion of the findings in proper perspective. The report reviewed relevant literature on estimates of sexual abuse and exploitation perpetrated by other professionals and the greater society. However, without valid figures on priests or critical evaluation of the sources of estimates on other populations, the report's concluding remarks were misleading. In addition, as with the John Jay College study and the National Review Board's reports, insufficient consideration was given to age- and gender-related differences and circumstances contributing to abuse. Likewise, along with most of the other Catholic-generated analyses, the author made unsupported assumptions about offenders' sexual orientations based on the gender of the victims.

In the past several decades, professional associations, licensing boards, and independent researchers have studied populations of helping professionals who hold similar statuses and privileges as religious leaders in serving vulnerable members of society. These include doctors, social workers, mental health professionals, and educators who work with both children and adults. Although discrepancies in research methodologies, definitions of sexual offenses, and areas of focus on the problem prevent statistical analyses of data across populations, a critical review of the findings from each of these professional groups and the greater U.S. population offers a broad comparative context in which to assess the scope of the problem in the Catholic Church.

Figures from the U.S. Department of Justice and the Census Bureau can be compiled to ascertain the percentage of adult men and women from the general population who were reported to the police for sexual offenses against minors or other adults during a time period similar to that used in the John Jay College study. This renders estimates that can easily be compared with the findings of other studies on individual subpopulations. Descriptions of the research methods and estimated figures on the U.S. population and each of the subpopulations to be discussed here are presented in what follows. Tables 2.1 and 2.2 display an organized summary of these estimates based on victim reports of abuse to authorities and on surveys of perpetrator or victim populations, respectively.

Catholic Priests and Nuns

The John Jay College study (2004) by far offers the most detailed statistics on child sexual abuse perpetration in any subpopulation that has ever been studied. Researchers collected survey data from 97 percent of the dioceses and 60 percent of the religious communities of men in the United States, representing 98 percent of diocesan priests and deacons and 80 percent of religious order priests in the United States from 1950 to 2002. The results indicate that 4.0 percent of all priests (4,392/109,694), 4.3 percent of diocesan priests, and 2.5 percent of religious order priests were credibly accused of sexually abusing children and youth during the years 1950 to 2002. If the time

TABLE 2.1. Estimated Prevalence (percentage of population) of Sexual Perpetration Based on Reports to Civil or Church Authorities

Population	Juvenile Victims	Adult Victims
Catholic Priests and Nuns		
Total	—	—
Priests total	4.30	—
Diocesan priests	5.00	—
Religious order priests	2.70	—
Nuns	—	—
U.S. Adult Population		
Total	1.29	1.05
Men	2.50	2.14
Women	0.15	0.02

TABLE 2.2. Estimated Prevalence (percentage of population) of Sexual Perpetration Based on Surveys

Population	Juvenile Victims	Adult Victims
Catholic Priests and Nuns		
Total	—	—
Priests	8.4[a]	30.5[a]
Nuns	0.7[a]	9.0[a]
Protestant Clergy		
Total	—	—
Men	—	12.7-37.2[b]
Women	—	—
Psychotherapists		
Total	0.2[c]	4.4
Men	<0.5[c]	7.0
Women	<0.1[c]	1.5
Educators (Psychologists)		
Total	—	12.6
Men	—	19.0
Women	—	6.0

[a]Study samples were drawn from a psychiatric subpopulation and data for adult victims include all reports of sexual contact contrary to vows of celibacy.
[b]Behavior ranges from sexual intercourse with a church member to sexual behavior inappropriate for a minister.
[c]Perpetration estimates were extrapolated from data on victim sample.

period is reduced to 1960-2002, the percentages increase to 4.3 percent for all priests, 5 percent for diocesan priests, and 2.7 percent for religious order priests (pp. 3-4). Because only forty-one permanent deacons (a category of lower-ranking clergy who are allowed to marry) were accused of sexual offenses against minors, the researchers simply included them in the statistics on diocesan priests. Most of the reported sexual abuse incidents occurred during the 1970s and 1980s but were not officially reported until the 1990s or later. About two-thirds of the victims were age twelve or older, and only a small percentage of priest offenders were responsible for multiple victimizations of young children. Only a quarter of alleged perpetrators were reported to the police, and about a third of them were sent to treatment facilities specialized in serving priests and religious men and women.

One such facility, the Southdown Institute located near Ontario, Canada, has treated thousands of religious men and women over several decades. Southdown conducted its own study of the sexual behavior of its residents over a twenty-five-year period through the use of a standard entrance survey (Loftus, 1999; Loftus and Camargo, 1993). Their researchers discovered that an average of 8.4 percent of its male residents admitted to having sexual contact with minors. For residents who entered treatment after 1991, the rate of perpetration jumped to 23.6 percent. According to the John Jay College study, of all the priest offenders reported to church officials in the United States, only 113 were sent to the Southdown Institute for treatment. Thus, we cannot assume that alleged priest offenders were over-represented in the Southdown sample due to administrative referrals.

In addition to those in treatment at Southdown Institute who admitted to sexual contact with children and youth, another 30.5 percent of male residents reported having inappropriate sexual contact with other adults (Loftus, 1999; Loftus and Camargo, 1993). This figure is similar to the findings of the *Los Angeles Times* survey conducted in 2002, which found that about 30 percent of priests reported difficulty in adhering to their vows of celibacy at some point in their ministry (Greeley, 2004). It should be noted that neither study differentiated between adult sexual activity with "celibate" peers versus sexual exploitation of vulnerable adults. Because Catholic priests and religious are expected to faithfully practice sexual abstinence, any sexual contact is considered morally problematic within the faith. For the purposes of social science research, sexual behavior between adults is only defined as exploitative if it involves a violation of trust within the context of a professional relationship. Advocates for victims of clergy abuse argue that religious leaders hold privileged status in society regardless of their professional roles, and therefore any sexual relationship outside of the accepted standards of that faith may be termed as exploitation. Sipe (1995) adds that within Catholicism, there is such a pronounced power differential inherent in the celibate culture of priests that all sexual involvement with lay persons (including nuns) may be considered exploitative.

For situations in which both adults consent to a sexual relationship and there has never been an assumption of either professional or client roles, this argument is more difficult to support. Likewise, sexual relationships between "celibates" in which there are no explicit power differentials are possible. However, the elements of secrecy and shame in such relationships, regardless of power dynamics, can lead to devastating consequences for one or both participants, including undetected HIV infection, unwanted pregnancy, and loss of vocation.

In response to the scandal and questions raised about sexual perpetration by women religious, the former director of Southdown Institute, Donna Markham (2002), presented data from an *ad hoc* sample of women who were treated there between 1993 and 2002. Markham's study is the only published research that specifically explores the prevalence of sexual perpetration by women religious. She reports that of the files reviewed, 0.7 percent of religious sisters admitted to sexual contact with minors and 9 percent to sexual activity with other adults at some point during religious life. Again, there was no distinction made between adult sexual encounters with peers and sexual exploitation of vulnerable adults. Because the sample was drawn from a clinical population, Markham assumed that the true prevalence of offending among women religious would probably be much lower. However, because Markham's source of data relied on honest admissions of transgression without anonymity, it could also be assumed that her results *underestimate* the prevalence. In general, only one-third of all suspected sex offenders confess to perpetration upon evaluation (Abel and Harlow, 2001).

Chibnall, Wolf, and Duckro (1998) gathered surveys from 1164 American Catholic nuns concerning victimization experiences of child sexual abuse, adult sexual exploitation, and adult sexual harassment. In reports of childhood victimizations (N = 216), male perpetrators accounted for nearly all of the abusers, with 6.0 percent being clergymen. However, nuns were the perpetrators of 3.2 percent (7 cases) of childhood sexual abuse experienced by this group. The researchers did not specify female perpetrators other than nuns as indicated abusers. Of the nuns in the study sample who were sexually abused in childhood, 23.6 percent had never disclosed the abuse, and those who did, waited an average of 24.7 years before discussing the abuse with anyone.

Of the 383 incidents of adult sexual exploitation or harassment revealed by the nuns in this study, other nuns accounted for 44.9 percent of the perpetrators. It is likely that the occurrence of sexual exploitation and harassment within religious communities of women is even higher than this figure reflects given that many women who experienced sexual trauma while in the convent may have chosen to leave their religious communities. It is doubtful that many, if any, of the abuses disclosed in this study, especially those committed by other nuns, were ever reported to the police. The researchers found that, of the nuns who were sexually exploited as adults, those who were exploited by women were significantly less likely to have discussed the experiences with anyone.

U.S. Adult Population

To estimate the prevalence of sexual offending in the U.S. population in a way that would be comparable to the methods used in the John Jay College study of Catholic priests, I used information from the FBI Uniform Crime Reports, the National Incidence-Based Reporting System (NIBRS), and the U.S. Census Bureau. The John Jay College study collected information on the number of allegations reported to diocesan officials by victims or their advocates. Similarly, figures contained in the Uniform Crime Reports and the NIBRS are based on incidences of rape and sexual assault victimization reported to the police. Of the priests accused of abuse, only a small percentage received allegations of abusing prepubescent children (John Jay College, 2004, p. 68). Likewise, most of the FBI data are on crimes involving victims aged twelve and older. Also, similar to the trend of reporting within the Church, reports of sexual offenses in the general population were highest between the years 1980-1995 (U.S. Census Bureau, 2003, No. HS-23).

During those years, law enforcement officers made a total of 2,122,071 arrests for forcible rape and other sex offenses (FBI, 1995). About 25 percent of those arrested probably had at least one prior arrest for a sex crime during that fifteen-year period (Greenfeld,1997; Langan, Schmitt and Durose, 2003), and so it can be estimated that three-fourths of the total number of arrests made represent individual sex offenders. According to the National Incidence-Based Reporting System, 67 percent of all sex crimes involve juvenile victims, and adult perpetrators account for 76.8 percent of those offenses. Male perpetrators are responsible for 94 percent of reported sex offenses against minors and 99 percent of reported sex offenses against adults (Snyder, 2000). Of all rape and sexual assault victimizations that are reported to the police, only 29 percent of crimes against juveniles and 22 percent of those against adult victims ever result in arrests (Snyder, 2000). Thus, the number of reported offenders may be up to 3.4 or 4.5 times greater than the number of arrests made for crimes against juveniles and adults, respectively.

To arrive at units of analysis that would be comparable to the data reported in the John Jay College study, I applied all of these percentages to the total number of arrests made for rape and sexual assault from 1980 to 1995. The results estimate the number of adult sexual offenders, male and female (169,438), who were reported to the police for crimes against juvenile and adult victims during those years. Each of these respective figures was then divided by the total population of males and females who were already adults or who reached adulthood during the period 1980-1995. These population figures were gleaned from Statistical Abstracts (U.S. Census Bureau, 2003, No. 11) by adding up the approximate number of males and females aged twenty and older in 1980 and those aged thirteen to twenty-four in 1990. This calculation method yielded estimates that 1.29 percent of all adults (2,823,924/219,286,800), 2.50 percent of men (2,654,526/106,213,800), and 0.15 percent of women (169,438/113,074,000) in the United States were reported to the police for rape or sexual assault of youth aged twelve and older during the years 1980-1995.

Rapes and other sexual offenses involving adult victims are all but 4 percent accounted for by adult perpetrators. Of these perpetrators, 99 percent are male (Snyder, 2000). Again, these percentages were applied to the estimated number of offenders reported to the police and divided by the population of adult males and females during the years 1980-1995. Based on this calculation, it was estimated that 1.05 percent of all adults (2,291,837/219,286,800), 2.14 percent of men (2,268,918/106,213,800), and 0.02 percent of women (22,918/113, 074,000) in the United States were reported to the police for sexual offenses against adult victims during this sixteen-year period.

One of the major limitations of the methods used to calculate these estimates is the inability to determine how many of the reported offenders may have been responsible for multiple victimizations that were reported but did not result in arrest. For this reason, these figures may be considered *overestimates* of the total percentages of men and women reported for sex offenses. Though the estimated prevalence figures rendered in these calculations are not exact, they offer a preliminary basis to refute the speculation that sexual abuse by Catholic priests and nuns is no more prevalent than sexual abuse in the general population.

Protestant Clergy

A number of studies on sexual misconduct by Protestant ministers have focused on adult sexual exploitation of parishioners, but have not identified child sexual abuse as a major subject for investigation. Consequently, we have no reliable estimates of the prevalence of child sexual abuse by Protestant clergy to compare with Catholic equivalents. The only publicly cited study on Protestant ministers that includes any exploration of child sexual abuse is a six-year study of the Presbyterian Church conducted in eight states, in which researchers found that out of seventeen reported cases of sexual misconduct by clergy, there were thirty-one victims, all female, and only one was a minor at the time of the abuse (as cited in Simpkinson, 1996).

Several other authors writing about the Catholic sexual abuse scandal (Berry, 1992; Bruni and Burkett, 2002; Catholic League, 2004; Jenkins, 1996; Kaiser, 1996) and attempting to offer a comparative context for priest abuses have quoted a statement made by G. Lloyd Rediger, a Presbyterian minister and counselor, that "about 2-3 percent [of clerics] are offenders" (1990, p. 55; 2003, p. 57). It seems, however, that Rediger's statement was misinterpreted and inappropriately quoted. The statement made by Rediger was a parenthetical comment that does not make specific reference to research on Protestant clerics and appears to be simply a generalization of estimates concerning pedophilia among Catholic priests. Upon my request for clarification from Rediger directly, he could not confirm a source for his figures, and instead directed me to other sources of information regarding sexual misconduct by Protestant ministers in general (personal communication, December 16, 2004). Unfortunately, no one has been able to reliably estimate the percentage of Protestant clerics who have abused minors because specific research regarding child sexual abuse by this population has not yet been conducted.

Much more rigorous attention has been given to sexual exploitation of adult parishioners by Protestant clerics. Blackmon (1984) surveyed ministers from four prominent Protestant denominations in southern California, inquiring about a variety of personal issues, including sexual experiences. Surveys were returned by 300 male participants (25 percent response rate) representing Presbyterian, Methodist, Assembly of God, and Episcopal denominations. As a collective group, 37.15 percent of the participants reported having sexual behavior inappropriate for a minister and 12.67 percent reported sexual intercourse with a church member other than a spouse. No significant differences between denominations were found related to any of the sexual misconduct variables. In addition, no statistical differences were found between self-identified theological orientations (liberal, middle-of-the-road, and conservative) for those who engaged in sexual intercourse with a parishioner. Blackmon's study was replicated in 1991 in a larger context by the Fuller Institute of Church Growth and found similar percentages for sexual behavior inappropriate for a minister and for sexual intercourse with a church member other than a spouse (as cited in Headington, 1997). Unfortunately, the measure of inappropriate sexual behavior remains vague as to whether the behavior was exploitative in nature. In addition to this study, Francis and Turner (1995) reviewed a number of smaller studies that also presented estimates based on self-report surveys. The figures ranged from 5.8 to 19 percent of Protestant ministers who admitted to inappropriate sexual behavior with church members. All of these studies have emphasized adult women as the victims of sexual misconduct by male clerics.

It is clear that there is a well-established problem of sexual exploitation within Protestant denominations from both the professional literature and popular media accounts. What is unclear is how extensive the problem is and how often minors are involved. More comprehensive research in this area is certainly indicated, though it appears that Protestant denominations have made further advances in addressing adult exploitation by their clergy than the Catholic Church has, even though Protestants have no expectations of clerical celibacy.

Psychotherapists

Kenneth Pope has been conducting research and writing about sexual ethics and exploitation by mental health professionals for the past few decades. He recently published a meta-analysis of eight national self-report surveys conducted from 1977 to 1994 in order to establish the best estimate of sexual exploitation by therapists in the United States to date. His results estimated that 4.4 percent of all psychiatrists, psychologists, and social workers have sexually exploited clients or former clients at some point in their careers. By gender, 7 percent of the male therapists and 1.5 percent of female therapists reported sexual perpetration. None of the studies used in Pope's meta-analysis distinguished between sexual abuse of minor clients and exploitation of adults. In addition, Pope estimated that 88 to 92 percent of therapists' victims were female (Pope, 2001).

In a separate study, Pope and Vetter (1991) found that, out of 958 adult clients who reported sexual contact with a previous therapist, about 5 percent were minors at the time of the abuse. Previously, Bajt and Pope (1989) had determined that, of the cases of therapist-minor client sexual abuse known to psychologists, 56 percent of the victims were female and 44 percent were male. The average age of female victims was 13.7 years with a range from 3 to 17. The average age of male victims was 12.5 years, ranging from 7 to 16.

In order to liberally estimate the percentage of all therapists who have sexually abused minors, I used the figure of 5 percent juvenile victimizations from Pope and Vetter's (1991) study of clients who were exploited by their therapists and multiplied it by Pope's (2001) percentage estimates of therapist perpetrators of victims of all ages. Noting that victimization rates are usually much higher than perpetration rates yielded by surveys and that most offenders usually have multiple victims, the resulting figures should be higher than what surveys of therapists regarding abuse of minor clients would be expected to yield. Likewise, since we have no information on the gender of therapists who may have abused minors, the full 5 percent was applied to each gender subgroup of therapists. The resulting products estimate that no more than 0.2 percent of therapists (0.5 percent of males and 0.1 percent of females) who reported having sexual contact with clients abused children or adolescents.

Educators

Empirical research on sexual misconduct by educators has relied almost exclusively on the use of surveys of students regarding victimization experiences. Once again, this methodology gives a better idea of the extent of harm done rather than the prevalence of offending by educators and school personnel. Consequently, no reliable estimates of perpetration prevalence for primary- and secondary-level educators are available. However, Charol Shakeshaft (2004) recently conducted a comprehensive review and analysis of the existing professional literature on this topic for the U.S. Department of Education. The most rigorous nationwide study to estimate prevalence of victimization indicates that 6.7 percent of all students in grades eight to eleven (7.6 percent of females and 6.2 percent of males) reported unwelcome sexual advances involving contact by a school employee at some time during their years of school attendance. Professional educators, including teachers, coaches, counselors, or principals, accounted for 57 percent of these offenses (Shakeshaft, 2003). Applying this percentage to the overall prevalence gives us an estimate that about 3.8 percent of the students surveyed were sexually abused by a professional educator. This estimate is similar to the percentage found in a 1986 study by Cameron et al. (as cited in Shakeshaft, 2004) in which 4.1 percent of adult survey participants reported having a physical sexual experience with a teacher as minors. Shakeshaft and Cameron et al. both found that male educators were responsible for about 57 percent of offenses and females perpetrated about 43 percent. If these studies' figures are accurate, this could mean that female-perpetrated abuse in schools is dramatically underreported to law enforcement officials (Shakeshaft, 2004).

Regarding exploitation of adult students by college instructors, again, very little of the research has examined rates of perpetration rather than victimization. Cleary, Schmieler, Parascenzo, and Ambrosio (1994) surveyed students at a large state university and found that, out of 292 students who returned surveys (26 percent response rate), 7 percent of both male and female students reported experiencing sexual advances or explicit propositions from faculty. In a 1979 survey of psychologists, Pope, Levenson, and Schover (1979) found that overall 12.6 percent of psychology educators and teachers (about 19 percent of males and 6 percent of females) and 4 percent of clinical supervisors (6 percent of males and 4 percent of females) reported having sexual contact with a student or supervisee at some point in their careers. In a later survey of psychologists, Lamb and Catanzaro (1998) found that 3.2 percent of psychologists (5.0 percent of males and 1.2 percent of females) reported sexual boundary violations with either students or supervisees. These various figures from over the years may indicate that the incidence of sexual exploitation by academic and clinical educators in the field of psychology has declined in the past two decades with increased awareness and prevention efforts. For the sake of comparison with the estimates of adult exploitation in other populations, the 1979 survey represents the time frame most similar to surveys of the other populations discussed here. Therefore, the highest estimates are entered in Table 2.2.

CHARACTERISTICS OF CATHOLIC SEXUAL ABUSE

Is Religion a Factor in Sexual Perpetration?

Gebhard et al. (1965) of the Institute for Sex Research conducted a groundbreaking study of incarcerated sex offenders that has served as the foundation for all subsequent research on this population. Their study sample included 1,356 white male participants who were incarcerated for sexual offenses against "children" aged eleven or younger, "minors" aged twelve to fifteen, and "adults" aged sixteen or older (p. 16). Among numerous other variables, the researchers measured participants' religious observance not only by affiliation but by level of devoutness. The study was designed with two control groups to compare the sex offender sample to other white male prisoners who were not sex offenders and to the general population of white men in the United States. The sex offender group was further divided into categories by type of offense, including nonviolent heterosexual offenses, heterosexual aggressive offenses, incest, homosexual offenses, peeping, and exhibitionism.

Regarding religious affiliation, Gebhard et al. (1965) found that Protestants, Catholics, and other religious affiliates were represented similarly in the total group of sex offenders and in the group of other prisoners as they were in the general control group, with the exception of Jews who were slightly underrepresented in both incarcerated groups. More recent studies have also found that child molesters, as a whole, match the U.S. population in education, marital status, and religious affiliation (Abel and Harlow, 2001; Elliott, D. M., 1994; Finkelhor, 1984). Regarding level of devoutness, Gebhard et al. found that the sex offenders, as with the other prisoners, were generally much less devout than their matched controls from the general public. However, they also discovered some remarkable exceptions for specific categories of sex offenders regarding both religious affiliation and degree of devoutness.

Gebhard et al. (1965) discovered that Protestants, particularly Pentecostals and "hardshell" Baptists and Methodists with low education levels, were disproportionately overrepresented compared to Catholics and other religious affiliates among incarcerated perpetrators of heterosexual incest. In addition, Protestants who committed incest with their older adolescent or adult children were much more religiously devout than Protestants in the general population. Since this study, other researchers within and outside of the United States have also linked Christianity and conservative family values to the occurrence of incest (Elliott, D. M., 1994; Imbens and Jonker, 1992; Williams-Morris, 1994).

Among incarcerated sex offenders who committed homosexual offenses against younger children and youth, Gebhard et al. (1965) found that Protestants and Catholics were proportionately represented, but that Catholics were more likely to have offended against children aged eleven or younger, while Protestants were more likely to have offended against older youth. What is most striking and relevant to the current discussion is that Catholics who molested same-sex children were also more likely to be moderately or highly devout than Catholics in any other group in the study (Gebhard et al., 1995, p. 49). Further study of these observations should be critical to any research and analysis of sexual abuse perpetrated by Catholic priests and religious as they represent a highly devout subset of the Catholic population.

Is the Sexual Abuse Crisis Only an American Problem?

Despite the Vatican's attempts to blame the sexual abuse crisis on American culture, which the Vatican spokesman, Joaquin Navarro-Valls once called "a society that is irresponsibly permissive, hyper-inflated with sexuality and capable of creating circumstances that can induce into grave moral acts even people who have received for years a solid moral formation and education in virtue" (as cited in Rossetti, 1996, p. 17), it appears from recent media reports and personal accounts shared in online discussion groups that sexual abuse by Catholic priests and nuns is as prevalent in other parts of the world as it is in the United States. Other industrialized countries where Catholics are concentrated, including Ireland, Canada, Mexico, and Australia, have also experienced similar nationwide scandals related to discoveries of horrific abuses in Catholic schools, seminaries, convents, and orphanages.

Even before the era of industrialization and mass media, sexual abuse scandals have plagued the Roman Catholic Church in Italy at least since the sixteenth century. Richard Sherr (1991) was able to reconstruct from archives the details of a sexual abuse scandal in Florence in the year 1570 arising from a tragic case involving a cleric who sodomized a young choirboy. Similarly, Judith Brown (1986), a history scholar from Stanford University, recovered archival information about a series of ecclesiastical investigations from 1619 to 1623 involving a nun in Vellano, Italy, who, as abbess of a newly established convent, used spiritual rhetoric to secretly coerce a young, illiterate nun into an exploitative relationship that lasted two years. The practice of pederasty (sexual relations between men and older boys) by clergy was condemned and harshly punished in the Church since the earliest centuries of Christianity, and the sexual abuse of minors by clergy was criminalized in canonical legislation at least since the fourth century (Doyle, 2003; Doyle, Sipe, and Wall, 2006). Though we have no way of knowing how prevalent the problem of sexual abuse by clerics was at different points in history, the fact that it is repeatedly addressed in canon law from various time periods signals that this problem is neither new nor isolated to modern American culture.

It may be that the problem of priests molesting children was allowed to reach epidemic proportions in the United States because of

American bishops' attempts to cover up abuses to avoid scandal. It may also be that this problem has festered for centuries throughout global Catholicism, but has finally reached a point of international attention because of the United States' unique status as a world leader. Some have suggested that the scandal in the United States became the focal point of the sexual abuse crisis not because the problem is any more prevalent here but because certain qualities of the American culture have made public exposure more probable. If there is one thing about American culture that defines it, it is this country's insistence on accountability from its leaders. Especially in the last few decades, Americans have grown skeptical of people in positions of authority, and church leaders are no longer the exception. Added to this factor is the profit-driven media in this country that could not bear to miss any opportunity to take advantage of the public's shock over such blatant hypocrisy in the nation's largest religious denomination.

PERPETRATOR CHARACTERISTICS

Before launching into a description of personal characteristics of Catholic religious perpetrators, I would like to draw attention first to the similarities in offenders' social situations and in the progression of sexually abusive scenarios. Most of the priests reported to officials for sexually abusing minors were well known and trusted by their victims' families (John Jay College, 2004). I have observed the same to be true in situations of abuse by nuns, based on my own experience and personal accounts from other victims or survivors. These priests and nuns were allowed to take youth alone into unsupervised situations or on spontaneous outings that served no official purpose. Often, the offenders played the role of substitute parents to their victims either because they were actively or passively offered the role by the victims' parents or because their victims were in the custody of Catholic institutions. Indeed, the role of surrogate parent may be the single most common characteristic shared by Catholic religious offenders of youth, making the dynamics of the abuse more similar to incest than other types of sexual offenses.

Common themes in the progression of sexual abuse include an initial grooming process, isolation of the victim or victims, spiritual justifications for personal boundary violations, and shared shame regarding sexual arousal and behavior. The grooming process is a common feature of sexual abuse by most child molesters, male or female (Hislop, 2001; Pryor, 1996). Adult offenders offer special attention to prospective victims, whether with conscious intention of molestation or as a product of their narcissistic needs for admiration. Once a child returns the desired emotional gratification, the offender progressively introduces physical and sexual contact. With religious offenders, the grooming process is usually characterized by a spiritual theme. Religious artifacts such as prayer cards, saint medals, and rosaries are used as gifts to seduce the child with religious mystery. Physical contact may be initiated in the context of praying together and is eventually paired with sexual arousal, fantasy, and gratification.

Religious sex offenders often use the context of prayer or attending to the spiritual needs of youths to isolate individuals or groups of potential victims from their peers and families. Once these youths are perceived by their social groups as either having special status with the religious minister or as having unusual religious interests, they may be alienated by their peers, contributing further to emotional isolation. As the sexual abuse is introduced, the offenders rely on this isolation to ensure secrecy. There is also evidence to suggest that religious offenders distort their perceived status with God and their theological beliefs to justify or excuse their exploitative behavior (Saradjian and Nobus, 2003).

Another common theme in religious sexual abuse is that perpetrators often express to their victims tremendous ambivalence and shame about their own sexual arousal and behavior. Sometimes perpetrators even apologize for or justify their arousal before or during the molestation, only to blame their behavior on their victims once the sex act is complete. If the victim experiences any sexual pleasure during the molestation, the perpetrator's shame is then shared with his or her victim. In this way, the perpetrator can twist his or her thinking to excuse the exploitative relationship as a mutual endeavor.

Personal characteristics of sex offenders that are often noted in research as different from the normal distribution of characteristics in the general population include gender, age, identified sexual orientation, history of childhood abuse, and various psychological or behavioral problems. The typical adult sex offender is male, between the ages of eighteen and thirty-five, heterosexual, married or formerly married, has a history of some form of childhood maltreatment, and consistently demonstrates antisocial behavior and poor impulse control. Among Catholic religious offenders, priests are more likely to be indicated as perpetrators than nuns, as we would expect based on the general gender trend. Likewise, priest offenders report similar histories of childhood abuse as other sex offenders when they are directly compared (Haywood, Kravitz, Wasyliw et al., 1996). Unlike typical sex offenders, however, most priest offenders are thirty-five years old or older when they commit their first alleged offenses (John Jay College, 2004), have never been married, and generally demonstrate high standards of social competence and self-control.

Another approach to discussing sex offender characteristics is to classify them according to the age and gender of their target victims, motivations to offend, level of social dysfunction, number and frequency of victim offenses, use of physical force, and whether they offend within or outside of their own families. While terms such as *pedophile* and *ephebophile* are commonly used to distinguish perpetrators of young children from those who molest postpubescent youth, these terms usually refer to individuals with a consistent, primary erotic attraction to children and do not necessarily imply criminal behavior as much as sexually deviant arousal. Likewise, not all criminal child molesters are pedophiles or ephebophiles. Rather, it is generally thought that child molesters fall somewhere on a continuum in their level of fixation on children as objects of sexual interest (Knight and Prentky, 1990; Schwartz, 1995). Abel and Rouleau (1990) report that about half of all child molesters exclusively target victims of a specific minority age group, while others are more flexible regarding the age of their victims, depending on access. Research on priests who molest children indicates that priests are more likely to offend against older children, have fewer victims, target male victims, and demonstrate less antisocial behavior but greater sexual conflictedness than other child molesters when directly compared (Haywood, Kravitz, Grossman et al., 1996; Haywood, Kravitz, Wasyliw et al. 1996; Langevin, Curnoe, and Bain, 2000).

Historically, men who sexually abuse their own children or stepchildren have also been thought to differ somewhat from other sex offenders. Studies suggest that most incestuous fathers are less fixated on children as primary sex objects, but that they easily regress to the point of sexual contact with children during times of stress, emotional insecurity, social isolation, or chemical intoxication. Compared to other sex offenders, incestuous fathers are generally older, have fewer victims, demonstrate less antisocial behavior, and are less sexually deviant, but may be more likely to have difficulties with sexual dysfunction, poor social skills, and isolation (Williams and Finkelhor, 1990). At this point, it appears that most priests who sexually abuse minors have more in common with incestuous fathers than with extrafamilial child molesters, though there is considerable overlap between all three groups. The two characteristics that most distinguish priest offenders as a group from both incestuous fathers and extrafamilial child molesters are that they rarely have experiences of marriage and that they most often abuse male victims.

As a unique population of perpetrators, female sex offenders have received much less attention in empirical research than male offenders, primarily because there are so few who have come to the attention of authorities. Of the female child molesters who are identified in professional research and literature, most are reported to have abused their own children or children for whom they have caretaking responsibilities (Elliot, 1994; Jennings, 1994; Rudin, Zalewski, and Bodmer-Turner, 1995). As with incestuous fathers, the same trends of having fewer victims, less antisocial behavior, and a later onset of sexual offending have also been observed for women who molest children compared to male offenders in general, whether they abuse within or outside of their own families (Jennings, 1994; Matthews, 1994; Wakefield, Rogers, and Underwager, 1990). However, female sex offenders are more likely to participate in sexually abusive behaviors in conjunction with male accomplices than are male sex offenders (Hislop, 2001; Jennings, 1994; Matthews, 1994). In addition, a majority of female perpetrators report having been sexually abused themselves in childhood (Jennings, 1994; Schwartz and Cellini, 1995) and often are also abused as adults by their male partners (Hislop, 2001). In the identified cases of child sexual abuse by female offenders, victims are more often girls than boys (Jennings, 1994; Rudin, Zalewski, and Bodmer-Turner, 1995).

To this date there are no published studies specifically addressing the characteristics of nuns who have molested children. However, from personal accounts it appears that nun offenders may be typical of female perpetrators who act alone in committing their offenses, and like priest offenders, they have more in common with incestuous parents than they do with sex offenders in general. Also similar to priest offenders and other female child molesters, it seems that the majority of nun-abuse victims are of the same sex, based both on media accounts and on the high number of nuns reporting childhood victimizations of sexual abuse by other nuns (Chibnall, Wolf, and Duckro, 1998).

VICTIM CHARACTERISTICS

Though the most frequently reported cases of sexual abuse by priests involve boys aged eleven to fourteen (John Jay College, 2004) and cases of abuse by nuns have not been systematically investigated, it appears that victims of sexual abuse and exploitation by Catholic religious men and women represent every age group and gender. They are young children, adolescents, and vulnerable adults all who looked to the Church for spiritual guidance and emotional support in various situations and for many different reasons. The religious authority figures of the Church represented the highest images of God on Earth to these victims, higher even than their own parents. Attention and special treatment from such figures were experienced by these individuals as much more than simple flattery, as a manifestation of God's unconditional love and grace bestowed on them by His specially chosen servants. To then have this experience of love and grace turned into a manipulative instrument of sexual gratification, a human impulse that they had been taught to disdain, was not only psychologically traumatizing but spiritually devastating.

Among the victims are females of all ages, the prey of priests and brothers who exploited their positions of trust for a moment of sexual pleasure. These victims are girls whose parents trained them well to be always quiet and accommodating, especially when Father is visiting. They are young teens who experienced their first crushes on men who treated them like princesses for as long as they were the one in favor. And they are women who were disillusioned with the empty promises of life and love they once expected, who turned for one last dose of hope to the only men who seemed to truly understand their needs.

There are young male victims of men who were once their role models, men they could trust and respect in an uncertain world that seemed desperately in need of passionate visionaries. These young bucks and older adolescents, full of vim and vitality, sought to share their wonder and to explore the mysteries of the world with priests and brothers who offered a fresh perspective on politics, nature, civil rights, and the quest for knowledge and spiritual fulfillment. Instead, what was modeled for them is that man's most important goals in life involve sexual indulgence and interpersonal dominance.

Similarly, Catholic school girls and young women, searching for a place to find the deeper meaning in life, an alternative to the limited roles cut out for them by their families and society, looked to the nuns and to the convents for emotional reassurance, safety, leadership, and spiritual community. But just when they started to blossom into their own potential as young leaders, many (like me) were tragically pushed back by their perpetrators' narcissistic demands that they remain firmly in positions of submissive admirers and sexual toys.

Finally, there are the countless young victims, male and female alike, of sexual humiliation, oppression, sadistic torture, and gross misinformation and condemnation regarding their natural sexual development while in the charge of nuns, priests, and brothers who were their teachers and guardians in Catholic institutions and missions. Some of the most explicit and chilling examples of these kinds of abuses were depicted in the controversial film, *The Magdalene Sisters* (Higson and Mullan, 2002). Writer-director Peter Mullan based the film on interviews with women who as teenage girls were placed in a Catholic asylum run by nuns in Ireland in the 1960s and were forced to work in a laundry facility for no compensation under the auspices of spiritual reform for sexually provocative behavior. Despite criticisms of the film by the Vatican, one need only read a few of the hundreds of personal accounts of abuses in orphanages and other Catholic institutions that have been widely publicized in newspapers and on the Internet to know that there must be some degree of validity to these allegations.

Also included among the victims of sexual abuse by Catholic religious leaders are the families of children and adult victims who were sexually exploited. There are untold numbers of children conceived in the context of sexual exploitation and then abandoned by their priestly fathers and destined to live their lives as bastards of the

Church. There are the parents who entrusted the Church with the care of their children for whom the level of trauma, grief, and betrayal experienced after finding out that their children were sexually violated can be as devastating as the abuse itself is for the immediate victim. Likewise, for many of the spouses, life partners, and family members of adults who were sexually abused either as children or vulnerable adults, the long-term effects on the victims also pose problems in family functioning and relational intimacy. The emotional roller coaster that many victims experienced when the scandal was publicly exposed has since become a source of relational conflict, emotional withdrawal, and a looming fear that life will never go back to the state of normalcy that they once enjoyed together.

SUMMARY

Current research suggests that Catholic priests and nuns may be more likely to sexually abuse minors than professionals in similar positions of trust or men and women in the general population. Along with Protestant ministers, Catholic priests and nuns may also be at greater risk of sexually exploiting other, more vulnerable adults. While the focus of scandal related to sexual abuse and exploitation by priests and other Catholic religious has been centered primarily in the United States, reports of similar abuses have been heard around the globe.

Past research on sex offenders suggests that religious devoutness may be a unique risk factor for Catholic sexual abuse of same-sex children. More recent research on clerical sex offenders and the findings of the John Jay College Study present the average priest perpetrator as older, more highly educated, less psychiatrically disturbed but more psychosocially maladjusted than other sex offenders from the general population. It appears that the majority of priests and nuns who sexually abuse minors have more in common with incestuous parents than they do with other types of sex offenders. Likewise, their offenses more often resemble the dynamics of incest than the patterns of compulsive, fixed pedophilia.

Victims of sexual abuse by priests and nuns are represented in every age group and gender. However, the cases of child sexual abuse by priests most often reported to church officials involve male victims of age eleven to fourteen. We currently have no empirical data on specific offenses, victims, or perpetrator characteristics of sexual abuse and exploitation by Catholic nuns, brothers, or lay ministers, though anecdotal evidence suggests that they may be similar to those of priests.

Chapter 3

Political Attempts to Identify a Singular Cause

Speculation about what caused the sexual abuse crisis in the Catholic Church has given rise to various reductionist analyses based primarily on the political views of the speculator. Initially, many defenders of the faith claimed that anti-Catholic propaganda and media sensationalism were to blame for the crisis. These attempts to deny that sexual abuse in the Catholic church is a significant problem have been seriously challenged by the results of the John Jay College (2004) study, which exceeded even the most liberal estimates presented by journalists before the study was conducted. Issues such as mandatory celibacy, homosexuality in the priesthood, and the power structure of the Church hierarchy have since become popular explanations for the crisis. These speculations have prompted both secular and ecclesiastical debate about how each of these issues may have contributed to causing the crisis, and what should be done to address it.

In an attempt to piece together a more comprehensive understanding, the National Review Board for the Protection of Children and Young People (NRB, 2004) conducted interviews of over eighty individuals they deemed "knowledgeable" about the issue of sexual abuse by priests, including church leaders, active and former priests, victims of clergy abuse, and lay professionals. One bishop, reflecting on the degree of bias associated with popular debate, commented to the interviewers, "If you're conservative, homosexuality is the problem; if you're liberal, celibacy is the problem. So tell me who you are, and I'll tell you what the problem is" (p. 64).

Sexual Abuse and the Culture of Catholicism

doi:10.1300/5633_03

This chapter will review the most popular of these theories as well as the findings of the NRB study. Many of the identified factors in these theories may have interacted to compound the problem of sexual abuse by priests; however, none of them alone can account for the prevalence and characteristics of sexual abuse perpetrated by both priests and nuns as outlined in the previous chapter. Thus, these factors are more likely to be *correlational* to the problem of sexual offending by priests and nuns rather than *causal*. Attempts to prevent problematic behavior by controlling co-related factors may have limited success, but without addressing the root causes, the problem may only be temporarily suppressed, allowing it to resurface again in the future without prediction. It is possible that the co-related factors identified in these preliminary analyses share a common underlying cause with the sexual abuse crisis, though it may be less apparent. A critical examination of these factors may offer clues as to what this underlying cause might be. It is only after full consideration of multiple factors operating on multiple levels within the Church that we can hope to prevent sexual abuse by religious leaders with any measure of efficacy.

CELIBACY

One of the first questions to arise during the clergy sexual abuse scandal was about how the unique status of priests as vowed celibates may have been related to the reported abuses. It seemed obvious to some people who enjoy an active sex life with their mates that something must be wrong with men who are committed to living a life of celibacy. Either they were defective to begin with or they became defective by trying to live a life that is "not normal." At the heart of this curiosity lies the question: does sexual abstinence cause some people to become sexually abusive? The answer, in short, is no. There is no evidence from research to suggest that refraining from sexual activity or intimate contact directly leads to inappropriate sexual behavior.

Some opponents of mandatory celibacy, however, have proposed that it is the level of loneliness and lack of personal intimacy that may lead some priests to seek out alternative means of meeting affectional needs. This may very well be true, particularly for diocesan priests who often live and work alone, but it does not logically follow that children, inexperienced youth, or vulnerable adults would become the primary objects of these lonely celibates' affections. While any mature adult may experience transient sexual interest in persons who are inappropriate for intimate partnering, socially functional adults also have conscious psychological barriers that prevent them from pursuing such interest. Instead, they may seek out intimacy with peers who are of equal power status and who share mutual interest and consent. Indeed, many priests and nuns have left religious life to pursue healthy adult relationships after realizing that they could no longer enjoy personally fulfilling lives in the priesthood or convent. Research on priests has shown that the majority of those who stay in the priesthood are happy with their lives and do not struggle significantly or consistently with their vows of celibacy (Greeley, 2004). Satisfaction and adjustment in priesthood is especially high for heterosexual priests (76 percent), who would be most affected by a change in the celibacy requirement, and somewhat lower for homosexual priests (53 percent), who are prohibited from marrying whether in priesthood or out.

More sophisticated arguments claiming that the celibacy requirement for priests and religious is what caused the sexual abuse problem are based on two assumptions. First, it is assumed that a celibate lifestyle may attract some candidates to religious life as a means to avoid confronting sexual difficulties (NRB, 2004). These difficulties may include sexual dysfunction, fears of intimacy, or homosexual orientation. Secondly, it is assumed that unresolved sexual difficulties will ultimately result in deviant behavior, including child molestation and sexual exploitation of vulnerable adults. Richard Sipe (1995) has added to these arguments by stating that the requirement of celibacy has contributed to the evolution of a power-driven clerical culture reflective of the psychological and sexual deficits of the individuals it attracts. The solution to the sexual abuse crisis, according to these arguments, would be, first, to develop better methods of screening out deviant candidates, and second, to abandon the celibacy requirement so that priesthood would become less appealing to undesirable candidates while also increasing new vocations.

These arguments fail to recognize that current research on adult sex offenders indicates that most of them are either married or formerly married at the time they commit their offenses (Abel and Harlow, 2001). Simply having access to appropriate sexual partners does not prevent sexual abuse or exploitation from occurring. However, it is reasonable to anticipate that opening priesthood and religious life to married individuals or couples would increase the overall population of nuns and priests simply as a function of less restrictive admission criteria. Second, observations of an elite culture of clericalism as a contributing factor to sexual exploitation may be quite accurate, but simply opening priesthood to married men may have little or no effect in changing that culture. Certainly, men in positions of power have been known to sexually exploit their status despite having wives. Finally, while better screening measures for candidates may reduce the number of seriously disturbed individuals entering seminaries or convents, research indicates that most clergy sex offenders exhibit only mild levels of psychiatric disturbance compared to other sex offenders. If admission criteria in this area became even more restrictive, then it is likely that some other restrictions would have to be reconsidered in order to address the already desperate need for new vocations. Perhaps for this practical reason, abandoning the celibacy requirement might be helpful, even if it is only minimally effective in reducing the overall number of priests and religious who sexually offend.

HOMOSEXUALITY

To many conservative Catholics, the most obvious factors seeming to contribute to the sexual abuse crisis are the infidelity of priests and excessively liberal attitudes on the parts of bishops and religious leaders. They argue that American seminaries and religious communities have been allowed to stray too far from traditional Catholic values and teachings, particularly regarding homosexuality (Dreher, 2002; Fox-Genovese, 2003; Hartigan, 2003; Lowery, 2002). From this perspective, the age and level of harm done to victims who have been abused by priests and nuns is less relevant than their gender and the fact that so many of our religious leaders have fallen into homosexual indulgence, corruption, and deceit. They see the real crisis in the priesthood as largely a problem of promiscuous gay priests having sex with underage but older adolescents. They point to Vatican II, the sexual revolution and the assimilation of Humanism into pastoral practice, as having contributed to a *laisser-faire* attitude toward homosexuality. Superficially, it would appear to some that gay priests and lesbian nuns are the ones who have strayed the farthest from traditional Catholic teachings and that they are the ones who are most inclined to sexually abuse victims of the same gender. Berry (1992, 2002) augments this argument by adding that liberal tolerance of homosexually active priests among the clergy has created an air of secrecy among clerics that serves to shelter gay priests who are active with minors.

This assumption—that priests and nuns who target same-sex youth for sexual abuse are gay—has become widely accepted by conservatives in the Church, despite protests and warnings from experts to the contrary (Allen, 2003a; Zoll, 2002). In November of 2005, Pope Benedict XVI reiterated this belief when he issued a statement banning men with deep-seated homosexual tendencies from entering the priesthood. However, gay or lesbian adults may be the least likely population to sexually abuse children in society (Jenny, Roesler, and Poyer, 1994). Even among men who abuse boys, Abel and Harlow (2001) found that "more than 70 percent of men who molest boys rate themselves as heterosexual in their adult sexual preference. In addition, 9 percent report that they are equally heterosexual and homosexual. Only 8 percent report that they are exclusively homosexual. The majority of men who molest boys are also married, divorced, widowed, or living with an adult partner" (p. 2).

Even those who know better than to directly suggest that gay priests are the root source of the problem point to a gay subculture (Berry, 1992, 2002; Cozzens, 2002; Lowery, 2002; NRB, 2004) or a "lavender mafia" (Dreher, 2002, p. 69) in seminaries as a contributing factor to the sexual abuse crisis. As a social worker who works regularly with minority populations, I am not at all surprised that a subculture of gay men exists in the priesthood. Minority subcultures exist in every diverse population on the planet. That members of this subculture tend to flaunt their differences with pride when they are together is common to minority groups struggling to overcome the negative effects of oppression by the dominant culture. To suggest that the sexual abuse of boys has been tolerated or even promoted in the priesthood because of the gay subculture that exists there is as simple-minded and erroneous as suggesting that the reason our prisons are overflowing with black men is because African-American cultural values, rather than poverty and oppression, contribute to violent crime. Have we not learned anything from the civil rights movement?

For those who defend their positions on excluding gay men from the priesthood by implying that an all-male environment is too much stimulation for a gay man to handle, their arguments are patronizing at best. This assumption is as tragically misinformed as a wife's fear that her husband will inevitably become sexually abusive of girls if he coaches his daughter's soccer team, or that he will undoubtedly have an affair if he joins his company's coed bowling league along with a few of his bachelor buddies. If there is reason to suspect malfeasance on the part of any priest or nun, then investigation and disciplinary action should be based solely on evidence of misconduct, regardless of the race, culture, or sexual orientation of the individual in question, and with all subjective biases in check.

It seems that a large number of heterosexual seminarians and priests have voiced concern about the growing number of openly gay priests. Part of this concern is that the obvious presence of a gay subculture creates conflict in seminaries and discourages new heterosexual candidates from entering the rapidly dwindling ranks of the priesthood. Another part of the concern is that if homosexual men are so easily welcomed into the priesthood, then the Catholic position on homosexuality as "intrinsically disordered" (Vatican, 1994, article 2357) may become more difficult to defend. Yet another fear is that gay cliques may offer political advantages to their members, resulting in discrimination against straight priests. It certainly would not be the first time that a "good-ole-boy" network participates in discriminatory practices but perhaps rare that heterosexual men would be the ones discriminated against. Again, this issue needs to be addressed as one of corruption and not as a factor of sexual orientation.

I am also not surprised that the number of gay men and lesbians entering seminaries and convents may be disproportionately higher than the number represented in the lay community. For devoted Catholics who wish to live in the full grace of the Church, the only acceptable options for adult lifestyles are marriage or celibacy. Whether conscious of sexual orientation or not, many older adolescents and young adults faced with the challenges of choosing a vocation and life partner must address how each of these choices will affirm their spirituality and enrich their personal development throughout their adult lives. It is not necessary that one is aware of being gay, bisexual, or straight at the time of discernment to know that one is not attracted to the lifestyle of heterosexual marriage. My guess is that the Catholic clergy and religious life have always had a high percentage of gay, bisexual, and lesbian members, but that these members have only recently had the language and support to identify themselves as such. Integration of one's sexual orientation into personal identity is a normal and healthy stage of all human development that usually occurs in adolescence. However, those whose orientations are considered disordered by their belief systems may experience delayed cognitive awareness and acceptance of their orientations until much later in adulthood, often as a component of midlife adjustment. Thus, it would also be expected that many homosexuals in the priesthood or religious life would not be fully aware of their orientations at the time they are discerning a vocation.

As a final note on this topic, I do not want my confrontation of false assumptions and heterosexual bias to be mistaken for negligence in attending to the role of homosexuality in the Catholic sexual abuse crisis. I do believe that the homosexual nature of the majority of the sexual abuse offenses reported, along with a disproportionate representation of homosexuals in seminaries and convents, are critical factors related to the problem but that homosexuality itself is not the cause. Along with other identified factors that may be related to this crisis, homosexuality needs to be explored from a well-informed perspective and with a neutral consideration of the data.

THE POWER STRUCTURE OF THE CHURCH

The third wave of speculation about what may have caused the sexual abuse crisis involves criticisms of the hierarchical structures of the Church that have contributed to corruption. As democracy gains favor throughout the world, many have questioned the practice of papal appointment of church leaders without input from the people over whom they are to govern. Many have drawn attention to the fact that bishops were originally elected directly by the people in the early centuries of Christianity. Their line of thinking is that if church officials were elected to office, perhaps, they would demonstrate greater concern and accountability to the laity, including victims of clerical sexual abuse, rather than acting solely out of loyalty to the institution. It has become widely recognized since the Boston scandal that this blind loyalty to protecting the image of the institutional church is what prompted many bishops to quietly relocate priest offenders and pay off their victims in exchange for silence. This practice certainly contributed to putting more children at risk and to allowing the problem to go on for so long without public awareness or intervention.

Berry (1992, 2004), Sipe (1995, 2003), Doyle (2003), and other analysts of the crisis have pointed to a culture of clericalism in the Catholic Church, which has offered members of the clergy unique social status and power within both the Church and society at large, as a major factor of not only the cover-up of offenses by clergy and bishops but of the sexually abusive behavior itself. This culture of clericalism may foster self-serving attitudes and narcissistic personality traits in sexually immature clerics who then act with a sense of entitlement in exploiting their positions of trust with the laity. This hypothesis is well supported by clinical evidence and professional literature describing the dynamics of sexual exploitation of vulnerable adults by clergy, psychotherapists, and health care professionals (Gabbard, 1995; Gonsiorek, 1995; Sipe, 2003).

Many church reformists have proposed that allowing for greater diversity within the priesthood and among church leaders may help to diffuse this elitist attitude and allow for greater representation of minority groups in church governance and decision making. Some advocates for reform have called for allowing women to become priests and for developing independent church councils made up of lay members to both assist clerics and ensure accountability. An additional benefit would be to help close the gap between a rapidly shrinking clergy and a growing church membership with increasing demands for service.

These analysts and advocates make several good points. The issue of a self-serving culture of clericalism operating in the Church helps to explain the higher rates of sexual exploitation of lay members by priests compared to other professionals and men in general. It also sheds light on the often reported "un-Christian" responses of church officials to victims of clergy and religious abuse. What this factor does not explain is why so many priests abuse pubescent and postpubescent boys. Another major issue that the culture of clericalism does not explain is the sexual offending of minors and adult women by nuns, who have never been included among the elite class of Catholic clergy.

NATIONAL REVIEW BOARD FINDINGS

In February of 2004, the National Review Board published their findings from a "comprehensive study of the causes and context of the current crisis," as they were so commissioned by the U.S. Conference of Catholic Bishops (p. 1). After interviewing selected Catholic religious and lay professionals with direct knowledge of sexual abuse by priests, the Board concluded that two sets of issues were at play in the evolution of the crisis: those related to screening and selection of candidates for priesthood and those related to how bishops responded to reported cases of abuse. Again, there was no consideration of abuse by women religious in their investigation, but many of the issues they identified may also apply to religious congregations of women.

Factors Related to the Selection and Training of Candidates

Assuming that potential sex offenders may be drawn to priesthood in the same way that they are to other vocations in society, the National Review Board identified poor screening and selection practices of diocese and religious orders as a primary factor contributing to the presence of perpetrators in the priesthood. They advised that candidates who are psychosexually immature may not be fit for a celibate lifestyle and that proper preparation for a life of chastity is essential. The Review Board also concluded that seminary formation on issues of sexuality was historically inadequate until the 1980s. They blamed lack of attention and discussion of sexuality in the 1940s and 1950s followed by a period of sexual confusion and relativism in the 1960s and 1970s for the equally unsatisfactory preparation of seminarians over four decades to deal with the challenges of the changing times (National Review Board, 2004).

While the Review Board was careful not to fault homosexual priests for the crisis, they did concede that homosexuality played a role in the crisis. They pointed to the fact that most reported cases of child sexual abuse by priests involved male victims and that, therefore, homosexual behavior was the operative factor in the abuse. Again, it should be noted that this logic is not supported by research, which indicates that more than 70 percent of men who molest boys identify themselves as exclusively heterosexual in their adult sexual preference (Abel and Harlow, 2001). The Review Board's report also included a description of the "gay subculture" that has been allowed to develop and flourish in some seminaries, "discouraging heterosexual men from seeking to enter the priesthood" and contributing to "an atmosphere in which sexual abuse of adolescent boys by priests was more likely" (p. 81). The Review Board therefore encouraged bishops who *choose* to ordain homosexuals to use "additional scrutiny" and "specialized formation" (p. 83). Since the release of this report, the Vatican has taken specific action to restrict the admission of gay men into seminaries worldwide.

Factors Related to Bishops' Responses to Reports of Abuse

In short, the National Review Board (2004) concluded that the U.S. bishops failed to respond properly to the sexual abuse of minors by priests. They blamed this failure on "moral laxity, excessive leniency, insensitivity, secrecy, and neglect" (p. 92). However, what the NRB described as the most fundamental aspect of the bishops' responses was the failure to understand the scope and appreciate the gravity of the problem of sexual abuse of youth by priests. In other words, bishops were in psychological denial about the reality of the crisis before them. This phenomenon was more fully described by the priest, psychologist, and former seminary director, Donald Cozzens (2002). Because of inadequate responses from bishops to remove any risk of re-offending by reported child molesters, the number of victims was allowed to reach epidemic proportions before external investigators exposed the crisis.

By admission, the NRB study was not conducted according to scientific methodology. To begin with, it only explored an internal, Catholic perspective and therefore did not take into account how the culture and beliefs of Catholicism itself may contribute to sexual abuse. In fact, the Review Board boldly proclaimed in the introduction of their report, "The problem facing the Church was not caused by Church doctrine, and the solution does not lie in questioning doctrine" (2004, p. 16). Likewise, their report offered no consideration of the possibility that the prevalence of sexual abuse in the Catholic Church may be significantly higher than in other areas of society. Finally, the study was limited to investigating only priests and deacons who abuse children and therefore failed to explore sexual exploitation of vulnerable adults or sexual offending by nuns, religious brothers, or lay ministers.

CONCLUSION

Well-intentioned Catholics from both conservative and liberal theological perspectives have attempted to isolate factors that may have contributed to the sexual abuse crisis in the Church. Speculations about what caused the crisis depend primarily on how the problem is defined. Initially, there were those who attempted to deny that the Church had a problem at all, aside from having to manage an anti-Catholic media frenzy. Since the figures from the John Jay College (2004) study were published, this argument has largely faded out of popular discussions.

More courageous and concerned Catholics have tried to face the crisis squarely but define the problem in various different ways. There are those who see the problem as one of predisposed pedophiles seeping into seminaries and convents because of poor screening practices and lax disciplinary policies. Some see the primary problem as a dwindling and lonely priesthood due to celibacy restrictions that put church leaders in desperate and compromising positions when addressing malfeasant clerics. Others see the problem as an issue of infidelity among priests and religious and the farce of a celibate clergy. Among these are some who believe promiscuous homosexuals are mostly to blame for seeking casual sexual encounters with older adolescents. Finally, there are those who see the problem as a narcissistic and detached culture of clericalism that has contributed to a wide range of exploitative vices, which may be easily tempered by allowing women and laity to serve greater roles in church governance.

While most of these explanations help to illuminate the issues, none of them directly account for the heightened prevalence of sexual offending against children and youth by both priests and nuns. Each of these attempts to explain the crisis offers clues to what may be underlying the sexual abuse problem in the Church, but they are limited in scope and depth. Most important, they are based primarily on subjective observations rather than controlled studies, making them prone to speculator bias. Yet people who are so emotionally affected by this crisis cannot help but try to figure out why it happened and how it can be resolved. This response is common in groups of people who experience sudden disruptions in the status quo. It is an automatic tendency to want to reduce immediate shock and anxiety by pointing to the simplest explanation. Unfortunately, this tendency often results in the most vulnerable members of the group being labeled as scapegoats for the sake of restoring temporary peace of mind for the group's most dominant members.

Six Reductionist Models Commonly Seen in Organizations

William White (1995), a noted consultant for organizations dealing with sexual exploitation, has identified six models of reductionist approaches to defining and addressing this problem, which fail to encompass the dynamic complexities of sexual exploitation either because they are based on erroneous assumptions or because they do not account for all contributing factors. Ultimately, these approaches either fail to prevent abuses or they fail to preserve the integrity of the organization. Each of the arguments described earlier can be identified in at least one of these reductionist models:

- The "Perpetrator Morality Model" identifies the source of all sexual exploitation as the inherent evilness of the perpetrator. Prevention therefore rests in learning to detect these "sexual psychopaths" and weeding them out of the organization. This is a simplistic and comfortable approach for those who wish to psychologically distance themselves from their own or other "normal" persons' potentials to offend.
- The "Victim Morality Model" serves a similar function but identifies the source of the problem in the proclaimed victim instead of the perpetrator. This model adheres to the belief that the victim is either flawed in some way that leads him or her to falsely accuse an innocent person of evil intentions or that they manipulatively seduced an otherwise respectable professional. In this model there is little concern for abuse prevention efforts because the problem itself is denied.
- The "Clinical Model" focuses on the related emotional or behavioral problems of the perpetrator, such as alcoholism, person-

ality disorders, or a history of family dysfunction, as the source of sexually inappropriate behavior. The solution then is to evaluate and treat individuals who have already offended or who may be "at risk." While this model holds truth and can offer some limited measure of success in minimizing the frequency and severity of abusive scenarios, it fails to address the dynamic social context of sexual abuse and exploitation, therefore failing to prevent new cases from developing.

- In the "Anomie Model," sexual exploitation is thought to result from the absence of clear ethical standards for professional conduct. This model assumes that any form of sexual exploitation is inevitable without explicit guidelines for behavior, ignoring the evolutionary process of the problem entirely.
- When sexual exploitation continues despite clear policies against it, the "Training Model" emerges. In this approach, organizations attempt to solve the problem of sexual exploitation through education and competency training for their employees.
- Finally, the "Environmental Model" explains sexually exploitative behavior as a fluke occurrence resulting from an idiosyncratic combination of factors in the perpetrator's immediate environment. In this model, the problem is addressed by simply relocating the offender to a different context. (White, 1995, pp. 177-180)

Rationale for Using a Systems Approach

Despite the limitations of the National Review Board's study, their findings offer a comprehensive overview of existing opinion from within the Catholic culture of the factors that may be related to the sexual abuse crisis, though none of them alone indicates what actually caused priests and nuns to sexually abuse youth at a higher rate than seen in other areas of society. However, both the stated conclusions of the NRB and their chosen methodology point to underlying organizational dynamics regarding issues of sexuality and authority in the Church that may create an environment that fosters sexual abuse. Conceptualizing the problem in the context of this environment offers an opportunity to explore further what may be at the root of the sexual abuse crisis.

Like White (1995), I propose using a systems approach in examining the problem. In this type of approach, multiple levels and factors are considered simultaneously as they interact within a dynamic social system. In the next two chapters, I will present a systems perspective of the Catholic sexual abuse crisis using an ecological systems model of sexual offending by Catholic priests, nuns, and other religious ministers of the Church.

Chapter 4

The Catholic Church As a Human System

Most social workers and family therapists would agree that the most effective approach in treating cases of child abuse and incest incorporates multiple levels of intervention focused both on safety for the victims and on preserving the family unit so that other critical psychological needs of the children can be met (Alexander, 1985; Cole, 1992; Friedrich, 1990; Hastings, 1994; Kemp, 1998; Maddock and Larson, 1995; Thorman, 1983). This approach is commonly referred to as *holistic* or *ecological* because individual needs are assessed and treated in relation to each other and within the context of the social environment. It is understood that the entire family must be helped in order to facilitate the health and well-being of each individual member. In taking an ecological approach, it is critical to understand both the origin and effects of abuse not only in terms of individual pathology but also as symptoms of dysfunction in the family as a human system.

Similar to a family, the Catholic Church also functions as a human system in society. The Church is frequently compared to a family because the central themes of love, communion, commitment, and transmission of moral values are central to each system's function and structure. Catholics refer to priests as fathers and to vowed religious ministers as sisters and brothers. This tradition reaches back to the earliest days of the Church with the Apostle Paul referring to himself as a spiritual father to the early Christians: "I do not write this to make you ashamed, but to admonish you as my beloved children. For, though you have countless guides in Christ, you do not have many fathers. For, I became your father in Christ Jesus through the gospel. I urge you, then, be imitators of me" (1 Corinthians 4:14-16, Revised

Sexual Abuse and the Culture of Catholicism

doi:10.1300/5633_04

Standard Version). Because of the similarities between the Church and families as human systems, applying the principles of family systems assessment and treatment regarding sexual abuse may offer new insight into the origins of the sexual abuse crisis and what interventions may be most effective to prevent abuse in the future.

WHAT IS A HUMAN SYSTEM?

Paul's description of the early Christian church as the body of Christ draws upon a very basic understanding of human systems theory: "For as in one body we have many members, and all the members do not have the same function, so we, though many, are one body in Christ, and individually members one of another" (Romans 12:4, Revised Standard Version). The study of general systems theory has often intimidated new students because the concepts appear to be very complex and abstract. The nomenclature itself can often add to confusion. For the purposes of this book, it will suffice to discuss only the most basic concepts of system organization, balance within the environment, and circular cause and effect.

The most fundamental assumption of systems theory is that the dynamic whole is greater than the sum of its parts. Imagine a three-dimensional mobile sculpture suspended in air. It is an arrangement of individual characters yet an object in and of itself. Its dual functions of movement and balance are interdependent and constantly affected by its environment. It may be hanging in a corner of the room as a unique work of art or displayed amidst a collection of other mobiles, allowing them to overlap and intermingle. It may be strategically hung within reach of a baby's crib, surrounded by a protective barrier in an art gallery, or suspended freely in open air.

The characters in a mobile respond in contagion to gentle breezes that may sweep over and between its parts. If the characters are allowed to come into contact with each other, they may create a chiming sound that is unique to each combination. With the touch of a finger to a single character, all of the characters dance around a single cord that joins them together and anchors them into place. As the mobile adjusts back into balance the character that was initially set into motion with a touch moves now in relation to the other characters rather than to the finger that touched it.

There are multiple levels and branches in a mobile that organize the characters into a hierarchy of connections of wire and thread to the central cord. Each branch and every character in the mobile is free to twist and move within a restricted range of space without touching or significantly affecting the others. The further away the branches and characters are spaced around the unifying cord, the greater the mobility of each character.

Similar to a mobile, a human system is composed of individual people or groups of people who function together as a unit within society. A common theme, such as family relatedness or political opinion, joins people together and anchors them into a particular space in the greater social context. A system may be situated in such a way that it is relatively isolated from similar systems or it may overlap with multiple other systems in society. Every human system is simultaneously part of a larger social system and a complete unit comprised of subsystems and individual members. Likewise, every person within a human system is also a complete system within him or herself, with biological, emotional, cognitive, and spiritual attributes. Each person in a system is connected to the whole through a network of communication, rules, and norms, analogous to the wires and threads of a mobile. When events occur in the larger system or environment, members of the smaller system must adjust in reciprocal contagion to adapt to the changes while maintaining balance around their centralizing theme. Adjustments within the system may happen rapidly if all members are affected simultaneously by a single event, or they may occur gradually and without notice to accommodate movement initiated in isolated areas over a long period of time.

As an illustration of these dynamics, consider the operations of a small dentist's office. Suppose that Melissa, the receptionist, gets a call one afternoon from a recent patient complaining that his temporary crown has come off. Melissa knows that the patient's permanent crown is available to be inserted and that the dentist, Dr. Benson, has an open appointment at the end of the day. Melissa offers the time to the patient and cancels the appointment he had originally scheduled later in the week to have the permanent crown inserted. When Melissa tells her office mates about the call from the patient and how she handled it, Dr. Benson explains that she will not be able to insert the permanent crown without Jenny, her assistant, there to help. Jenny then shares that she has already made plans to leave work early that day to meet her husband for a celebration of their first wedding anniversary. Dr. Benson suggests that Melissa call the patient back to confirm that she will secure the temporary crown that afternoon but that he will still need to keep his original appointment later in the week for his permanent crown to be inserted.

When Melissa gets in touch with the patient, he says he cannot keep his original appointment because he has already scheduled something else for that time, thinking it was available. Melissa then approaches her office mates again to see if Jenny would be willing to adjust her plans so she can stay to assist with the insertion of the patient's permanent crown. Dr. Benson agrees that Melissa's suggestion is the best solution, since the patient's needs should always come first. Jenny concurs but is resentful that she will have to change her plans. She does not express her feelings in front of Dr. Benson, but later pulls Melissa aside to tell her how angry she is. From then on, Melissa decides never to offer patients emergency appointments without first checking with everyone in the office to see if they plan to work regular office hours. This pleases Jenny but compromises the service standard that Dr. Benson had previously established with her patients, even without her knowledge.

Human systems are organized into subsystems based on power, function, and proximity to the unifying theme. Likewise, each person within a subsystem fulfills a particular role, which in turn allows the subsystem to function properly in maintaining balance within the entire system. If a single member acts in a way that is outside his or her expected role, the subsystem must adjust and the entire system is ultimately affected. For example, Ben plays receiver on his junior high school football team. If the quarterback throws a pass to Ben and he runs in the wrong direction, his own offensive linemen may quickly shift their positions to try to tackle him before he scores for the opposing team. Though the only players involved are members of the offensive line, the entire team is affected by Ben's confusion. The opposing team is also affected, as are the fans for both teams who attended the game. Every interaction between and within subsystems contributes to an intricate web of interdependent relationships between individual members. Every relationship is therefore influenced by both systemic functioning and individual member needs. And in turn, every relationship has an impact on each individual and every other relationship in the system.

Collectively, and as individuals within a human system, we regulate how much or how little the greater environment affects us and our relationships by creating external boundaries to protect the integrity of our system's structure. If conditions in the environment are perceived as threatening, the system may establish firm boundaries to limit the influence of both external changes and overlapping systems as a means of self-preservation. When the environment is perceived as nurturing and enhancing of the system's functions, external boundaries may become flexible and open to changes initiated from the outside. If the system's internal structure is weak, however, rapid changes in the environment may sever connections within the system, causing it to lose balance or to fall away from its anchoring theme and purpose, resulting in chaos and division.

Human systems grow and evolve over time, similar to how each of us develops and changes throughout our lives. Systems also go through developmental stages, experienced as either periods of rapid change or minor adjustments over a long stretch of time. Growth and development in human systems are continuously being affected by, and having effects on, their environments. For example, the high-tech Internet search engine company, Google, experienced rapid growth soon after its young cofounders, Larry Page and Sergey Brin, introduced their innovative product to Internet users. As the Internet grew in popularity, so did the demand for fast and accurate search capabilities. Eventually, the owners of the company decided to sell shares on the public stock market in order to finance its promising development. Though the action was initiated by the company, the effect was reciprocated by the environment. Google's evolution then became dependent not only on its function for consumers in society but also on the investments and demands of its stockholders. Google's future will also be determined by the actions of other systems in the environment, such as its major competitor, Microsoft. To accommodate sudden changes in the greater social environment, the strength of Google's infrastructure and communication have become critical.

The ins and outs of the business sector may not be so familiar to some, but everyone is acquainted with the most common human system in society, the family. Each family system is unique, but certain characteristics apply to all families. Every family is initiated by two adults who come together through sexual attraction and intimate bonding. The interpersonal dynamics and social situation of this primary pairing establish the unifying theme and structural characteristics of the couple. As children are added to the system, the relationships that form between parents and children and between siblings are greatly influenced by the primary relationship dynamics and norms established between the parents. Likewise, as the family grows and functions within society, environmental factors have an impact on the family system relative to the roles and qualities of the relationships established between individual family members. The development and behavior of each individual child is thus influenced by multiple systemic and environmental factors they must adapt to in order to maintain balance around the central, unifying relationship between the parents. In return, the developmental needs of the children demand continuous change and adaptation from the parents, influencing the evolution of their primary relationship.

Social scientists have applied the principles of systems theory to study families for several decades now. Through this application, we can now identify and describe common traits of families that function well in society and in which its members tend to be well adjusted and psychologically healthy. We also have a useful framework to assess and treat families that are not functioning well or in which members must struggle to meet their individual needs through maladaptive efforts while accommodating the balancing needs of the system's hierarchy. It easily follows, then, that using the analogy of the Catholic Church as a family can offer a common language and familiar context in which to examine the dynamics of system dysfunction, particularly related to sexual abuse. We will start first with an examination of characteristics of functional, sexually healthy family systems and then contrast them to the dynamics of sexually dysfunctional family systems. Common characteristics will be explored in the Church's history and current functioning. This will be followed by a direct comparison between a family dealing with incest and the Catholic Church's handling of the sexual abuse scandal of 2002.

Sexually Healthy Family Systems

James Maddock and Noel Larson (1995) present an ecological model for understanding sexually healthy families in contrast to sexually dysfunctional families. They begin by clarifying several assumptions about the common characteristics of family systems. The first assumption is that sexuality, as a fundamental aspect of all human existence, plays a major role in family life. It is an essential motivator in bringing couples together and transmitting life to a new generation. It affects how families are organized around gender roles and influences the psychosexual development and pleasure-oriented activities of individual family members both within the family unit and in relation to the greater social environment.

Another common characteristic of families that Maddock and Larson (1995) describe is the dynamic tension between power and control among individual members and between the family system and the outer social and material landscape. This dynamic tension creates boundaries that define and regulate the capacity for influence of each member in relation to another and of the family as a whole in relation to its environment. The "power/control dialectic," as the authors describe it, has traditionally been divided in families based on gender roles and position in the family hierarchy.

In traditional families, men are expected to exercise personal power outside the home, in competition with other men for social and material resources. Within the home, male power goes unchallenged and wives are expected to exercise their own personal power in tending to the day-to-day needs of the household and in teaching moral values and discipline to the children. Even in today's less traditional families, where the focus is more on affectional bonds rather than on survival, the functional roles of earning family income and taking responsibility for child rearing often fall disproportionately between parents according to gender. While this gender-linked division of roles has worked very well in most families, we have learned from history that sharp differences in power between the genders has made women and children more vulnerable to abuses by men and at significant disadvantage in functioning independently in society as single-parent households.

The other way that power and control are expressed in family relationships is between the generations. The authority of parents is assumed based on the dependency of children, although children have a tremendous influence on the lives of parents, even before they are born. In functional families, parents coordinate their use of power and control to protect their children from potential harm and to influence healthy physical, emotional, cognitive, and spiritual development. Older generations pass on cultural beliefs, family traditions, and rules of behavior, whether consciously or not, that have served them well in their own lives.

The established patterns of interaction within a family system regarding sexuality and power and control dynamics determine how well the system functions in meeting the biological, cognitive, emotional, and spiritual needs of each member while maintaining harmony between members and within the greater environment. Maddock and Larson (1995) describe five general criteria regarding gender-linked power, personal boundaries, communication, sexual beliefs, and social interaction that characterize family sexual health:

- *A balanced interdependence among all family members based upon respect for both genders as legitimate and valued,* including their physical embodiment and their ways of experiencing and conceptualizing reality—regardless of perceived similarities and differences between males and females
- *A balance between boundaries that defines individual family members* and that maintains suitable physical, psychological, and social boundaries relevant to their respective ages and stages of the life cycle—while supporting appropriate gender socialization and personal erotic development
- *Balanced (verbal and nonverbal) communication among family members* that distinguishes between nurturing, affection, and erotic contact while helping all of these to occur between appropriate persons in developmentally suitable ways
- *Shared sexual values, meanings, and attitudes among family members,* permitting a balance between shared family goals and activities, on the one hand, and individual decisions and actions, on the other
- *Balanced transactions between the family and its social and historical environments,* reflected in reciprocity between family members' sexual attitudes, meanings, and behaviors and those of their families of origin and their community (p. 64).

Sexually Dysfunctional Family Systems

In contrast to healthy families, sexually dysfunctional families have been identified and described by family systems theorists as either sexually neglectful or sexually abusive (Alexander, 1985; Friedrich, 1990; Hastings, 1994; Maddock and Larson, 1995; Thorman, 1983).

Both are characterized by gender-linked distortions in power and control dynamics and by conflicted expressions of sexuality. In sexually neglectful families, gender roles rigidly adhere to tradition without meaningful exploration of unique gender qualities or individual strengths. For the most part, external family boundaries are open but interpersonal boundaries are tightly controlled. Conflicts in power and control are typically expressed indirectly, resulting in passive-aggressive interactions and guilt-inducing disciplinary styles with children. Erotic feelings rouse anxiety and are generally suppressed. Expressions of affection are primarily directed toward children, especially infants and toddlers. Sexuality is never discussed with children and attitudes toward nudity and erotic interests of children and adolescents are shamefully restrictive. Even sexual activity between spouses is usually focused on procreative function and is mostly characterized by minimal communication and a lack of creativity (Maddock and Larson, 1995).

On the other end of the spectrum are sexually abusive families. These families are characterized by a dramatic imbalance of power and control between spouses and between parents and children. Male power and control dominate in the family, and females are expected by both genders to be cooperatively submissive. Marital discord or emotional estrangement between spouses, paired with poor communication, is almost always present in incestuous families. Failing to address the marital problems ultimately results in one parent, typically the mother, either physically or psychologically retreating from the family unit. Eventually, a child is groomed into a surrogate spousal/parental role on behalf of one or both of the parents.

Incestuous families have very rigid, closed external boundaries, keeping the family isolated from the greater social environment. As a result, the family suffers from a lack of critical feedback from the outside world, and members become dependent exclusively on each other to meet all personal and social needs, including sexual gratification and validation of personal power. Emotional resources are scarce in these families, and attempts to gain affection ultimately become competitive and sexualized. In order to manage emotional pain, defend against unexpressed shame, and avoid facing the devastating effects of their behavior, both parents and children rely on dissociation from feelings or psychological denial, often aided by substance abuse or elaborate cognitive distortions of reality.

THE CATHOLIC CHURCH AS AN INCESTUOUS FAMILY SYSTEM

Revisiting now the primary issues of debate raised in the wake of the scandal and those discussed in the previous chapter, the question remains as to what these various issues have in common that might point to a shared underlying cause. It is my assertion that the issues of increased prevalence of sexual abuse by priests and nuns, the failure of bishops and congregational leaders to fully face the problem, the frequency of same-sex offenses, the persistence of celibacy requirements for religious ministry, and the resistance to include women and laity in positions of leadership all share the same source: the sexual shame and dysfunction of Catholic leaders since the time of the Church's formation, which has in turn resulted in a persistent cycle of sexual neglect and incest affecting every level of the Church system. Throughout the history of the Church, oppressive sexual beliefs; rigid, idealized gender roles; and a shaming, patriarchal leadership style have operated within the social system of the Church, similar to the dynamics of incestuous families, to foster optimal conditions for sexual abuse to emerge and thrive among the Church's most devout followers. The sexual teachings and practices of Catholicism have created extreme ambivalence toward both sexuality and gender, the effects of which are most detrimental to those whose innermost passions are condemned.

Historic Roots of Sexual Shame in Roman Catholicism

A Brief History of Catholic Sexual Teachings

The Catholic Church's theological roots regarding human sexuality are based primarily on Aristotelian ideas about natural law, Stoic asceticism, and Old Testament emphasis on procreative sex as a means of populating the earth. Denial of human sexuality as anything more than a method of bearing children is at the core of most Catholic beliefs regarding sexuality. In addition, remnants of ancient Jewish legends regarding the female image as split between the asexual "Madonna" and the seductive "Whore" were propagated throughout much of early Christian thought (Schwartz and Cellini, 1995). In the earliest days of converting pagans to Christianity in anticipation of Christ's imminent return, the Apostle Paul focused on evangelical urgency in calling upon unmarried men to remain single for the sake of purity, focus, and mobility in spreading the word of Christ. Once Christianity started to proliferate in the Roman Empire, Greek philosophy and pagan traditions played a much greater role in theological developments of the early church.

The first theologians began writing in the third century in an effort to protect the faith from heresy. These early Christian writers shaped fundamental dogma on God, creation, "the nature of man" (and woman), divine grace, and the Holy Trinity. Many attributed "the fall" of Adam and Eve to sexual incontinence. Some even believed that Adam and Eve were sodomized by the serpent to force them into "an unnatural kinship with the animal world" (Brown, 1988, p. 95). Indulgence in sexual pleasure, like the animals, doomed us to mortality.

St. Augustine (AD 354-430) defined "original sin" as the inherent sinfulness of human nature passed from one generation to the next through the act of conception (Gonzalez, 1971). Augustine also wrote on the virtues of virginity, which he held as an ideal, though he himself was known to have multiple sexual partners, including a mistress who bore his child only to be cast away when Augustine betrothed a young girl who had not yet reached puberty (Bullough, 1990). Intimate relations between Mary and Joseph and the sexual interests of Jesus were left ambiguous in the gospels, yet Mary was declared by the Church in 431 to have had a virgin maternity, rendering an image of the ideal woman as simultaneously sexless and maternal, a biological impossibility. Likewise, the two natures of Christ were defined in 451, qualifying that Jesus was both fully human and fully divine in nature, yet the figure of Jesus was to remain asexual despite his humanity (Orlandis, 1985).

As Christian asceticism, influenced by stoic tradition, grew in popularity throughout the West, it eventually inspired the monastic movements of the Middle Ages. "Religious" ministers (members of monasteries, convents, and later religious congregations) began taking vows of chastity, poverty, and obedience (Orlandis, 1985). Scholastic theology was born at the end of the eleventh century and blossomed in the thirteenth century with Thomas Aquinas (1225-1274). The scholastic method combined divine revelation with reason and Aristotelian concepts of natural law (Gonzalez, 1971). Regarding sexuality, this influenced the development of church doctrine by church leaders that was based on their understanding of "natural order," including the superiority of men and "venereal activity" for the sole purpose of procreation. Any sexual activity that resulted in venereal pleasure without the intent of procreation was seen as unnatural or disordered and was therefore sinful. For example, upon considering "whether virginity is more excellent than marriage," Aquinas writes:

> Now, virginity is directed to the good of the soul in respect of the contemplative life, which consists in thinking on the things of God, whereas marriage is directed to the good of the body, namely, the bodily increase of the human race, and belongs to the active life, since the man and woman who embrace the married life have to think on the things of the world, as the Apostle says (1 Cor. vii. 34). Without doubt therefore virginity is preferable to conjugal continence. (1273/1948, p. 1809)

Similarly, pedophilia became theologically linked to homosexuality in Christian thought because both were perceived as unnatural distortions of the procreative purpose of sexual behavior. No attention was given to the social context or consequences of various sexual behaviors. Indeed, as Aquinas expounds upon the evils of lust, he explains how "procuring pollution" (spilling semen through masturbation or contraceptive practices) is a more grievous sin than incest:

> Therefore, since by the unnatural vices man transgresses that which has been determined by nature with regard to the use of venereal actions, it follows that in this matter this sin is gravest of all. After it comes incest, which, as stated above, is contrary to the natural respect which we owe persons related to us. (1273/1948, p. 1826)

Power Exercised Through Sexual Issues

Since the fourth century, when Christianity became the official religion of the Roman Empire, the Roman papacy has enjoyed political, intellectual, and moral authority over much of society. When the empire started to crumble, bishops began to be canonically appointed rather than elected by the people and clergy. Feudalism led to a moral corruption in the papacy through the manipulation of nobles and imperialists with secular interests. Popes were nominated by emperors before meaningless canonical elections. Monasteries flourished, as did clerical abuses including the buying and selling of spiritual ministries for personal profit and blatant nonobservance of celibacy rules (Orlandis, 1985).

The schism between the Greek East and the Roman West resulted in a split between empires in 1054. Suspicions of eastern influence in the West led to the creation of the Inquisition to combat heresy in 1478. Canon law was also developed and transcribed in the latter centuries of the Middle Ages. Celibacy of the priesthood became mandated during this time so that priests could not marry or beget heirs and were instead obligated to "perfect and perpetual continence" (Canon 277 1, in Sipe, 1995, p. 59). Though chastity was practiced as the ideal since the first century, priests were not canonically restricted from marriage until the thirteenth century.

By the end of the Middle Ages, Protestant revolts throughout Europe and a desperate need for reforms within Catholicism inspired spiritual renewal and a restructuring of the clergy, culminating with the Council of Trent (1545-1563). This Council resulted in a declaration that divine revelation was transmitted through both apostolic tradition and sacred scripture, as interpreted by the Church Magisterium (bishops, cardinals, and the pope collectively). Clergy were required to attend seminaries to prepare them to go out into the community to teach and minister directly to the people. With the discovery of new lands, including America, this movement developed into a period of widespread missionary work, especially under Spanish leadership. However, the political supremacy of Protestant powers, royal absolutism, and the French Enlightenment movement continued to weaken the authority of the papacy (Orlandis, 1985).

Pope Pius IX (1846-1878), resisting the erosion of his temporal authority, published two encyclicals, *Quanta Cura* and *Syllabus of Errors* (1864), attacking science, relativism, materialism, divorce, freedom of speech, democracy, and the competency of modern governments (Wills, 2000). The First Vatican Council (1869-1870) later supported this bold assertion of the intellectual and moral authority of the Church for all eternity through the proclamation of papal infallibility.

Following in Pope Pius IX's footsteps to defend the moral authority of the papacy, Pope Pius XI (1922-1939), in *Casti Connubii* (1930), condemned all practices of contraception, citing both natural law and scripture in a way that was widely considered erroneous by theological scholars of the day. Therefore, his effort only accomplished the reverse of his objective in scholastic circles, especially in America. American theologians who expressed dissonance were harshly disciplined, silenced, or excommunicated (Kennedy, 2002).

Pope John XXIII and Vatican II (1963-1965) later attempted to embrace modernity, offering, among other advances, the increased involvement of the laity in church ritual and governance. Unfortunately, John XXIII's efforts were soon thwarted by the actions of his successor. Fighting the indulgences of the sexual revolution, and the radical possibilities opened by Vatican II, Pope Paul VI fell into the same struggle to maintain the moral authority of the Church in his encyclical against birth control, *Humanae Vitae* (1968). The papal preoccupation with sexual issues as a means to assert the moral authority of the Catholic Church in society has carried through to today (Kennedy, 2002; Wills, 2000).

A lifelong commitment to chastity is still an ideal that the Church promotes. Religious leaders, in the monastic tradition, are expected to take vows of chastity, obedience, and poverty so that they are free from the distractions of earthly temptations in their service to God and the Church. Since it is recognized that this lifestyle is a difficult one, it is believed that only those who have been graced with a special gift from the Holy Spirit, a charism, should attempt it. If a person believes he or she has this gift, then it is considered a special "calling" to serve God and the Church in a unique and blessed way. It is not difficult to understand how this chosen group has garnered privileged status within the Church culture from the time of the early Christian fathers. Likewise, because the Church's official interpretation of scripture reveals that Jesus called only men to be his disciples, and because natural law according to apostolic tradition has maintained that women must serve a different role in God's kingdom than men, the Church firmly asserts that only men can be called to the sacrament of Holy Orders to become ordained priests.

Current Catholic Teachings on Sexuality and Gender

According to the *Catechism of the Catholic Church* (Vatican Congregation for the Doctrine of the Faith, 1994), sex outside of marriage, including premarital sex between engaged couples is strictly prohibited, as it is "gravely contrary to the dignity of persons and of human sexuality which is naturally ordered to the good of spouses and the generation and education of children" (article 2353). Therefore, those who are not married should be committed to a life of chastity. The church accepts only two divine reasons for sex: procreation and the strength of the bond between a husband and wife. In order to qualify for the sacrament of marriage, a couple must be open to "unity, indissolubility and fertility" (article 1664).

Likewise, all unnatural forms of contraception are strictly forbidden. Married couples are allowed to use natural means of birth control, commonly referred to as the "rhythm method," by abstaining from sex during the wives' fertile periods. However, "every action which . . . proposes, whether as an end or as a means, to render procreation impossible is intrinsically evil" (Vatican, 1994, article 2370). Hence, all methods that may be employed to prevent conception prior to the sexual act, such as the use of birth control pills; during the sexual act, such as the use of condoms; or after the sexual act, such as taking the "morning-after" pill, are rigorously prohibited. In the same line of reasoning, abortion as a means of birth control is considered to be profoundly evil and unquestionably illicit.

Similarly, homosexuality, as a lifestyle, is also condemned by the Catholic Church. While the Church recognizes the long-time existence of homosexual relations among its followers, the Church's persistent stand on the issue is that homosexual relations are "acts of grave depravity," "intrinsically disordered," and "contrary to natural law" (Vatican, 1994, article 2357). Despite the Church's calls for homosexual persons to be treated with respect and compassion, noting that homosexuality is not a choice of the individual, the *Catechism* commands homosexual persons to a life of chastity, as "sexuality is ordered to the conjugal love of a man and a woman" only (article 2360). Thus, gay and lesbian Catholics who wish to remain within the faith must put aside their intimate passions and remain solitary, as same-sex relationships are not in accord with Church teachings on conjugal love.

The place of women in the Catholic Church has seen some limited development over the last century. According to the *Catechism* (Vatican, 1994), men and women were created by God in "perfect equality as human persons" (article 369). Each was created as "an image of power and tenderness of God, with equal dignity, though in a different way" (article 2335). While the Church espouses that men and women are equal in dignity, they are also distinctly different and complementary in function. This dichotomy between the genders has placed females as a gift given to man "by God as a helpmate" (article 1605). It is this dichotomy in the function of men and women that has been the basis for the Church's exclusion of women from participation in the Church as clergy, since "the ordination of women is not possible" (article 1577).

Reflections on Catholic Sexual Theology

Ironically, Aristotle, who is credited with the theory of natural law upon which much of Catholic doctrine is based, was not only the first Greek philosopher to apply reason to nature but he was also the first to use scientific methods in observing creation. He based his explanations of natural phenomena on empirical investigations rather than abstract reasoning alone. Observations of natural behavior provided information for his process of reasoning rather than his reasoning dictating what is to be considered "natural."

The Catholic Church's theology rests on Aristotle's conclusions without regard for to historical context. One might wonder how today's sexual ethics might have been different had early theologians not only embraced Aristotle's ideas but also his methods of empirical research as a means of interpreting divine revelation through creation. Instead, the Church has stifled scientific inquiry throughout history and still today rejects science as the primary means of understanding human sexuality and intimate behavior above the theological reasoning of ancient and medieval Christian writers. Thus, Catholic theology remains fixed on the science of the past, which was limited to observing God's creation as purely anatomical.

The result has been periodic outbreaks of symptoms from a systemic illness that has plagued the Church since the third century. Perhaps the true source of the original sin was not in the concupiscence of Adam and Eve, as Augustine believed, but in their sexual shame. The arbitrary exclusion of human sexuality from spiritual experience has established what Eugene Kennedy (2001) describes as an "unhealed wound" so deep and unshakable that its pain must be numbed with the intoxication of power. Kennedy poignantly describes this in his book by the same name, and summarizes the tragic effects for faithful Catholics:

> Countless people have been made to feel at odds with their own human nature and have, as a result, lived their lives in a sexually handicapped way, trying to follow institutional mandates and interpretations that by a perverse alchemy transform their naïve human eroticism into something base and evil. (p. 39)

Systemic Characteristics That Contributed to "Incest" in the Church

From an ecological perspective, the pervasiveness of sexually shaming beliefs, sharp imbalances of power between genders, stifled communication in church leadership, and rigid cultural boundaries that isolate Catholics from the rest of society have come together to create an atmosphere in the Church system that is conducive to incest. In seminaries and convents of the 1940s and 1950s, as in many Catholic parishes and family households, erotic interests were either denied or shunned. This was followed in the 1960s and 1970s by a period of confusion and relativism regarding sexuality (NRB, 2004). For many, who were discouraged by Pope Paul VI's conservative retreat from the progress of Vatican II, this led to disillusionment with the papacy and rebellious dissent among church leaders. Many priests and nuns left their ministry in the Church as a result, or they retreated from leadership positions into isolated pastoral roles. This period in church history was experienced systemically in a way analogous to marital discord and emotional estrangement between parents. Since then, little has been done to reignite communication and passion between the divided sectors of church authority and pastoral care, between the institutional church and the Church of the people.

Imbalances in power exist not only between "parents" of the Church but most obviously between males and females at every level in the Church system. Women are barred from becoming priests and from participating in positions of authority and decision making in the Church hierarchy. The less-than-covert message here is that females, as inherently powerful as they may be, are always inferior to males and should therefore accept submission willingly. Male power dominates so extremely within Catholicism that females, even as receptacles for male sexual pleasures, have been designated by church doctrine for the exclusive purposes of procreation. It is no wonder that, even among male Catholic child molesters, male victims are the preferred targets for erotic expression.

Finally, the Catholic Church's resistance to modern social sciences has left it isolated in a world that has grown beyond the Church's limited understanding of human development and interpersonal relationships. It is apparent not only in the Church's doctrine related to sexuality and gender but also in its style of governance. We know all too well since the clergy abuse scandal that the Catholic Church's tightly coiled patriarchal leadership style has disastrously failed to prevent an organizational nightmare.

THE 2002 SCANDAL: A CASE STUDY OF INCEST

In reflecting on the parallels between the Catholic Church and families as human systems, I have noted with interest that the Church's handling of the 2002 scandal was also very similar to how families typically react to the revelation of incest. It is common in families in which incest occurs for the nonabusing parent to misread or minimize obvious signs of the incestuous relationship as it develops between the spouse and a child. In a typical case of incest in which a father abuses his daughter, the mother may suspect the abuse but clings to a state of denial in the interest of keeping the family together. She may feel torn between protecting her daughter from her husband's advances and enjoying the relief of not having to deal with him herself. Often the mother may become jealous of the incestuous relationship and grow to resent both her daughter and her unfaithful husband. However, the mother's emotional and financial dependency on her husband may keep her from recognizing her power and ability to change the situation. Overwhelmed and isolated, she ultimately chooses to ignore the problem so that she can maintain the sense of security offered by status quo. In other words, ignoring the problem allows the family system to remain in balance around the unifying theme, which, in this case, has become distorted by dependency. In the case of the Church and the sexual abuse crisis, we see both parents failing to communicate with each other, dispassionate about their partnership, and so consumed with their own problems and needs that they cannot effectively tend to the needs of their children. On the one hand, we have the "father" of the Church, represented by the clerical institution—powerful, demanding, and oppressively controlling of the family's sexuality. On the other hand, we have the pastoral "mother" of the Church—those in direct ministry who have become disillusioned with the Church hierarchy, yet are too passive and dependent to initiate significant change. As the two drift further and further apart, each becomes more isolated. Neither has sufficient social contact within the greater community to recognize alternatives, seek assistance, or otherwise meet their personal needs in appropriate ways outside of the Church "family." Both of these "parents" are at high risk for turning to their own children for immediate gratification of their suffering adult needs. The "father" may become more and more desperate to regain the feeling of unquestioned power that he once enjoyed from his wife and seek sexual gratification from whoever is most accessible as a means of reassuring his position of dominance within the family. Feeling rejected by her husband, the "mother" may become seductive with her own children, seeking both emotional comfort and reassurance of her sexual desirability. As the abused children grow up and leave the family, those who develop supportive resources in the greater community eventually recognize that their own family experience was not the same as what others experienced. The distress of this recognition ultimately leads them to reveal the abuse, whether out of rageful vengeance or out of loyalty to their younger siblings.

In 2002, the abused children of the Church finally reached a critical point in their own psychospiritual development. In connecting with each other and with supportive resources in the secular community, they revealed not only individual cases of isolated abuses by a handful of pedophile or ephebophile priests but a situation of incest and dysfunction affecting the entire church system. The events of 2002 and beyond reflect the typical stages of disclosure of incest by victims, attempts to intervene by community-based institutions, and the reactive effects of the disclosure on the family system.

The process of disclosure for victims of incest is often very complex and difficult. As we witnessed with the victims of sexual abuse by Catholic religious leaders, many do not come forward until sufficient support to do so is gained in the outside community. In families, victims of incest often wait until well into adulthood before revealing the abuse to only a single person whom they can trust with the family secret, often a therapist. This is a very frightening and confusing experience for the victim, and is commonly followed by a period of regret and attempts to minimize the abuse and defend the abusive parent. However, with appropriate support, the deeper trauma is eventually exposed. At this stage, the adult victim may then seek out support and information from other community resources, older or younger siblings, or other allied family members. As additional support and validation is secured, the incest is finally revealed to civil authorities, who investigate and intervene in the family system to stop the abuse from continuing with younger family members. In the case of the Catholic sexual abuse crisis, *The Boston Globe* reporters and other news journalists played the same role as investigative social workers in Child Protective Services.

Once incest in a family is exposed, it is common for both parents, whether active or passive in the abuse, to initially deny, minimize, or justify the incestuous relationship. A nonabusing parent is almost always expected to deny having any knowledge of or responsibility for the sexual abuse. As the details of incest unfold and the crime can no longer be denied or justified, the parents may align to try to excuse the sexually abusive behavior as an understandable consequence of an unforeseen factor, such as illness, unemployment, or a relapse of chemical dependency. They try to convince their social worker and the judge that the solution is simple and that they will fully comply with correcting this identified factor through direct action steps. This way, they reason, they can promptly and safely resume their family life as it was before the abuse occurred. We have seen this same pattern from the American bishops with their quick creation of the *Charter for the Protection of Children and Young People* (2002) and a prominent show of compliance through audits conducted by their own, hand-selected review board members.

In working with incestuous families, however, state authorities are not so easily convinced. Parental rights usually remain suspended while the children are in the care of trustworthy relatives or foster homes. Meanwhile, the parents are usually required to undergo intensive treatment to address individual psychosexual pathology and issues of conflict in the marital relationship. They also have to demonstrate significant and permanent changes in the structure of power in the family system in order to retain their parental rights. Even if all of these requirements are accomplished, and the children are returned to the parents' custody, Child Protective Services will continue to supervise the family until the children reach adulthood.

Unlike incestuous families, however, the Catholic Church answers to no other human authority beyond its own ancestors and elders. While secular authorities may have the power to intervene in individual incidences of abuse, they have no way of influencing the dysfunctional patterns of the system that continue to create new opportunities for incest to occur. Attempts to address the problem by the "grandparents" of the Church will likely result in a simple repetition of the same strategies that they used to address the problem in previous generations. We know from history that these strategies may appear to be effective for a while, instigating new movements in the system's dynamic balancing act. However, without restructuring the relationships within the system, correcting distortions in the unifying theme and creating openness to the greater social environment, these new movements will eventually settle back into the same patterns that resulted in incest before.

What we have witnessed within the Catholic Church since the sexual abuse crisis was revealed is reflective of a human system that has lost its balance, resulting in chaos, confusion, and power struggles between various subsystems. For the laity, as well as for many religious in the Church, it has become unclear where the internal and external boundaries lie, who are in the roles of authority, where the sources of comfort and nourishment have gone, and in what direction the Church needs to turn in order to restore functional harmony. Some members of the faith may even wonder whether the Catholic Church has fallen away from its unifying themes and purpose of promoting healthy spiritual growth and maturity for its faithful followers.

Chapter 5

Systemic Sexual Shame and Catholicism

In the previous chapter, we saw how the dynamics of the sexual abuse crisis in the Catholic Church resemble the dynamics of incest in a family system. Several factors from the social environment contribute simultaneously and on multiple levels to incest. In the current chapter, I will review the major theories that attempt to explain how individual characteristics also contribute to sexual abuse. Combining individual risk factors with an ecological perspective of the Church will allow us to explore more specifically how these factors may have come together within the belief system of Catholicism to cause the current crisis. I will present my own model of a cycle of sexual trauma, which incorporates systemic sexual shame as a source of childhood trauma and later dysfunction. Finally, I will apply this model to explore possible risk factors that may explain why Catholic priests and nuns may be at higher risk to sexually abuse minors than other men and women in similar positions of trust, and why Catholic religious offenders more often abuse youth of their same gender.

MAJOR ETIOLOGICAL THEORIES OF SEXUALLY ABUSIVE BEHAVIOR

Several theories of sexual offending and child molestation have been formulated throughout the twentieth century by biological, behavioral, and social scientists. Pedophilia was first classified as abnormal, among other sexually deviant behaviors, by the psychiatrist

Sexual Abuse and the Culture of Catholicism

doi:10.1300/5633_05

Krafft-Ebing in 1892 (Schwartz, 1995). Child abuse was later recognized as a social problem in many parts of the world due to the traumatic and lasting effects that it appeared to have on its victims. In the United States, Congress passed the Child Abuse Prevention and Treatment Act (P.L. 93-247) in 1974, which criminalized child neglect, physical abuse, sexual exploitation, and other forms of child maltreatment. Since then, public and private funding has become widely available for research exploring the causes of child sexual abuse so that prevention efforts may be more successful.

Biological Theories

Many theories about sexual deviance in general have focused on genetic, hormonal, chromosomal, or neurological factors that may be responsible for aberrant sexual behavior (Schwartz, 1995). Certain aspects of sexual attraction and arousal are simply a product of genetic variability occurring in nature (Feierman, 1990). Since the vast majority of pedophiles and criminal sex offenders who are apprehended by police are male, chromosomal and hormonal factors have also been explored by scientists for specific effects. In addition, physiological factors related to alcohol and substance abuse and neuropsychopathology may also contribute to sexual offending (Feierman, 1990; Hucker and Bain, 1990; Langevin, 1985, 1990; Lothstein, 1999; and Schwartz and Cellini, 1995).

Cognitive-Behavioral and Social Learning Theories

Cognitive-behavioral and social learning theories have considered the effects of childhood and adolescent learning experiences on sexual arousal and behavior in adulthood. Through the repeated pairing of sexual stimulation and gratification with deviant sex objects or themes, including sex with children, sex offenders may develop preferences and impulses that they continue to act upon in adulthood (Laws and Marshall, 1990). Problematic arousal patterns may be further reinforced by exposure to pornography (Murrin and Laws, 1990) or through the repeated pairing of sexual gratification with anxiety, power, or humiliation (Carnes, 1991; Darke, 1990).

Cognitive processes regarding sexuality may also become distorted by immediate social factors and beliefs (Segal and Stermac, 1990). Similarly, feminist theories maintain that sociocultural values such as male supremacy, negative attitudes toward women, tolerance of interpersonal violence, and the psychological submission of women, children, and youth, also contribute to broad-scale sexual exploitation of women and children by men (Herman, 1990; Stermac, Segal, and Gillis, 1990).

Psychoanalytic and Developmental Theories

Psychoanalytic theorists originally conceptualized child molestation as an expression of arrested psychological development by which the perpetrator relates to children on the same emotional level and seeks age-inappropriate affection in an attempt to resolve unconscious childhood conflicts (Finkelhor, 1984; Thorman, 1983). Later, psychodynamic formulations emphasized the role of identification with the aggressor and/or mastery processes in traumatized childhood victims of abuse. There is some evidence to support that childhood victims may compulsively repeat the dynamics of their abuse, sometimes in the role of the perpetrator, in an effort to understand and resolve their traumatic experiences (Garland and Dougher, 1990).

More recently, attachment theory has been applied to describe the intimacy deficits of sex offenders that may originate in early childhood due to inadequate parenting during critical periods of development. Insecure emotional attachments to parental figures may result in later relationship difficulties that block their access to appropriate adult sexual partners, leading them to seek substitute affection from less threatening children and youth (Markham and Mikail, 2004; Ward, Hudson and McCormack, 1997).

Family Systems Theories

Developed out of approaches to family therapy in the 1970s and 1980s, systems theories have been applied primarily to explain familial incest patterns. In these approaches, the problem of incest is defined in terms of family dysfunction rather than individual pathology. From a systems perspective, parents and/or older siblings abuse younger children when marital conflicts, blurred boundaries, power imbalances, and poor communication exist in dysfunctional family systems that are socially isolated or closed off from community resources (Schwartz, 1995). Chapter 4 applies systems theory in comparing the Catholic Church to an incestuous family system.

More recent studies have also identified family environmental factors that may contribute to child sexual abuse in general. The most prominent factor that has been repeatedly identified in research is the absence or emotional unavailability of one or both of the victim's parents due to any number of circumstances including marital conflict or divorce, parental impairment, maternal illness, or substance abuse (Benedict and Zautra, 1993; Putnam, 2003). Social isolation and punitive parenting styles in families have also been associated with increased risk of child sexual abuse in empirical research studies (Putnam, 2003).

Cycle of Abuse

Criminal justices and mental health practitioners of the 1980s began noting that many sex offenders of minors also reported being victims of sexual abuse in their own childhoods. These observations evolved into a popular theory that sexual abuse may be transmitted through a cycle of abuse from one generation to the next (Hastings, 1994; Putnam, 2003). The abused/abuser hypothesis has been criticized by some because it does not account for the majority of childhood abuse victims who never commit sexual offenses as adults. However, while about 10 to 20 percent of men in the general population report histories of childhood sexual abuse (Garland and Dougher, 1990; Gartner, 1999), about 30 to 50 percent of adult male sex offenders report having been sexually abused in childhood (Abel and Harlow, 2001; Haywood, Kravitz, Wasyliw et al., 1996; Garland and Dougher, 1990; Gebhard et al., 1965). The prevalence of sexual abuse victimization in childhood among adult male sex offenders of male victims and adult female sex offenders of either gender appears to be even higher than it is among other categories of sex offenders (Garland and Dougher, 1990; Gebhard et al., 1965; Schwartz and Celleni, 1995).

Debate over the idea of a cycle of abuse has risen for the most part out of oversimplifications and misinterpretations of the relationship between childhood sexual abuse and later offending. The hypothesis does not attempt to predict the outcome of childhood sexual abuse victimization but rather attempts to explain how it may serve as one of many risk factors for later sexual offending. A number of retrospective studies on childhood sexual abuse have confirmed that the prevalence of victimization among people arrested for sex crimes and prostitution is significantly higher than it is in the general population (Abel and Harlow, 2001; Putnam, 2003). While this observation provides evidence of a strong relationship between having a history of childhood sexual abuse and sexualized criminal behavior, including sexual assault, the relationship cannot be assumed as one of direct cause and effect but as part of a sequence of possible effects (Garland and Dougher, 1990). Research also suggests that there are gender differences in how cross-generational transmission occurs, with men being more likely to sexually offend against children and women being more likely to fail in protecting their own children from abuse (Putnam, 2003).

Integrated Theories

The contributions of each of the theoretical perspectives described earlier are noteworthy. However, none of them alone can fully account for the causation of child sexual abuse. Many researchers and clinicians who work with sexual offenders have advocated the use of more complex, multifactor approaches to understanding why some adults molest minors. Integrated or ecological theories consider multiple levels of interaction between a potential perpetrator and the social environment to explain what ultimately causes a person to offend. David Finkelhor (1984) developed the most widely referenced model using this approach. He and his colleague, Sharon Araji, reviewed the major theories and relevant research and classified the identified risk factors for child sexual abuse into four general factors in the realm of the perpetrator: emotional congruence with children or youth, sexual arousal toward the victim, blockage from appropriate sources of sexual gratification, and disinhibition from committing the offense (Araji and Finkelhor, 1986). Each of these factors will be examined more closely in reference to sexual abuse by priests and religious later in this chapter, but first I will present a conceptual framework in which to consider these factors in the life of the perpetrator.

A MULTIFACTOR ECOLOGICAL APPROACH TO SEXUAL OFFENDING

By combining an ecological understanding of incest and sexual exploitation in human systems, with a consideration of the prominence of sexual shame in religious teachings, the contributions of major etiological theories of sexual perpetration, and my own personal and professional experience, I have developed a more comprehensive, dynamic model to conceptualize a cycle of sexual trauma. I believe this cycle, fed by systemic sexual shame, particularly related to homophobia, operates as the root cause of the sexual abuse crisis in the Catholic Church.

The Cycle of Sexual Trauma: A New Twist on an Old Idea

Cycle of Abuse versus Cycle of Trauma

Observations of a cycle of sexual abuse have proven to have some merit, but as the basis for a cohesive theory of perpetration, they are largely inadequate. One area of weakness in popular theories regarding a cycle of abuse is that they do not accommodate for variations in the level of trauma imposed on the victim by the circumstances of a particular event or by chronic or repeated victimizations. There are many possible outcomes and effects of childhood sexual abuse on the lives of victims, depending on any number of variables that may regulate or intensify psychological/sexual trauma. For instance, the victim's relationship to the perpetrator, the nature and duration of the abuse, the presence of religious or ritualistic themes, the extent of family support upon disclosure, and the individual victim's strengths and abilities to cope with trauma may all affect the presence and severity of later difficulties (Putnam, 2003; Rossetti, 1995). Thus, some individuals who experience childhood sexual abuse may recover with minimal intervention, while others who experience similar victimizations experience more severe and persistent pathological effects, depending on the level of sexual trauma imposed by the abuse.

Cycle-of-abuse theories are also limited in that they only apply to sex offenders who report histories of childhood sexual trauma resulting from abuse. Studies of clergy offenders report inconsistent findings regarding the prevalence of childhood sexual abuse in this population. Rossetti (1996) reports that about two-thirds of the priest offenders he has worked with in treatment were themselves victimized as children or adolescents. Langevin, Curnoe, and Bain (2000) found that only 12 percent of mixed Protestant and Catholic cleric sex offenders and 25 percent of noncleric offenders, who were matched for age and socioeconomic status, had experienced abuse. Haywood, Kravitz, Wasyliw et al. (1996) reported that only 21 percent of priest offenders were childhood victims compared to 50 percent of noncleric offenders, but that they were six times more likely to have been victims than matched cleric controls who were not sex offenders. Finally, the John Jay College (2004) study of reported priest offenses revealed that only 6.8 percent of the perpetrators had a recorded history of childhood sexual abuse victimization. It is clear that, while childhood sexual abuse may be a factor for some priests who offend, it does not play a role for a large portion of priest sex offenders who do not have a history of childhood sexual abuse.

Likewise, female sex offenders are thought to have a much higher prevalence of childhood sexual abuse than women in general or male sex offenders. There are a limited number of studies on female sex offenders, but preliminary findings suggest that at least three-quarters of the women who sexually abuse minors were also victims as children (Schwartz and Celleni, 1995). If nuns, as a group, are at higher risk for sexually abusing minors than other women, we might expect to find a higher prevalence of childhood sexual abuse histories among nuns. However, Chibnall, Wolf, and Duckro (1998) did not find that nuns were any more likely than women in the general population to have experienced childhood sexual abuse. This seems to indicate that something other than or in addition to childhood sexual abuse is at play in contributing to both priests and nuns becoming child molesters. Is it possible that they experienced sexual trauma as children or adolescents from something other than direct sexual abuse?

Sexual Shame As a Source of Trauma

In my own personal experience and in working with sexual minority and abused clients, I have learned that there are multiple sources of childhood sexual trauma that have tremendous impact on issues of sexual health and personal power. These other sources of trauma may not be readily identified as sexual abuse *per se* but as critical experiences of sexual humiliation, gender-based degradation, sexual neglect or gross misinformation, homophobia, stigmatization due to teenage pregnancy or sexually transmitted disease, and other forms of sexual disempowerment. Often, the sources of trauma associated with these experiences in childhood and adolescence stem from sexual shame and intolerance derived from rigid, conservative, religious, and cultural beliefs. I have worked with many clients struggling with adult intimacy conflicts and sexual compulsion issues for which early sexual trauma, unrelated to direct sexual abuse, played a significant role in the manifestation and persistence of difficulties. Other authors have written more extensively on the subject of sexual shame, or passive sexual trauma, as a source of many adult sexual disorders (Hastings, 1994, Kaplan, 1974; Prendergast, 1993, 2004).

To account for both direct sexual abuse and sexual shame as factors contributing to childhood sexual trauma, I have created a new scheme for conceptualizing a cycle of sexual trauma, rather than abuse alone, to explain the intergenerational transmission of traumatizing behaviors and effects. To begin with, Figure 5.1 illustrates a very basic side-by-side comparison between the old concept of a cycle of sexual abuse and the new model I am proposing of a cycle of sexual trauma. This model will be presented in much greater detail in the following sections.

The Experience and Effects of Sexual Trauma

Sexual trauma, like other forms of extreme stress, has a significant impact on every level of personal existence: biological, cognitive, emotional, and spiritual. When trauma is experienced in childhood or adolescence, it may disrupt developmentally sensitive neuronal, psychological, and behavioral processes that are critical to normal maturation. This disruption, in turn, affects the internal experience, social behavior, and interpersonal environment of the traumatized youth. Even with therapeutic healing of the psychological injuries inflicted by sexual trauma, the scars often remain throughout a lifetime.

Mechanisms of Sexual Trauma

The primary experience of sexual trauma is one of internal psychological and emotional conflict related to the victim's perceptions of the abusive or shameful situation. If children are abused or shamed by a major caregiver, they may initially experience extreme confusion

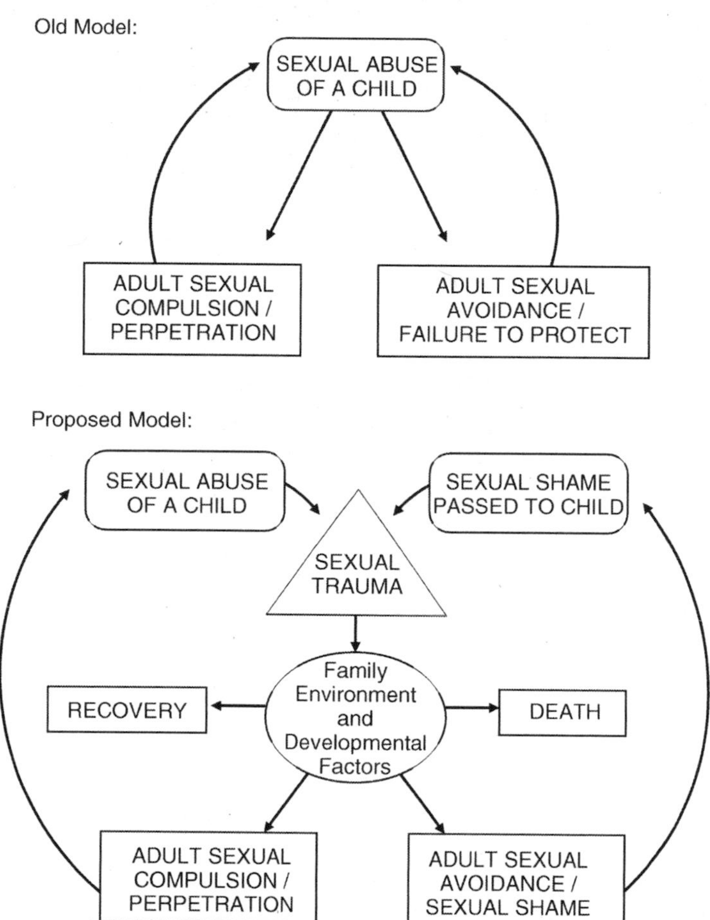

FIGURE 5.1. The Cycle of Sexual Abuse vs. The Cycle of Sexual Trauma

and a split in their perceptions of the caregiver that is then generalized to their overall world view. As a result, young children resort to blaming themselves for all that goes wrong in their lives rather than the overwhelming alternative of perceiving the world as unpredictable, corrupt, and unsafe. Older children and adolescents, however, who are dealing with issues of mastery and individual identity development, may struggle more with this split in their world views, vacillating between extremes of self-stigmatization and feelings of enraged self-righteousness regarding the unfairness of life. To manage these feelings on a day-to-day basis or to maintain socially acceptable behavior, traumatized youth must fracture various aspects of subjective experience into distinct areas of perception, which are then processed and stored in separate areas of the brain. By this process of fragmenting perceptions and awareness, the psychological defenses of dissociation and denial become embedded in the fabric of their developing personalities. For more detailed information on the nature of early childhood trauma and its specific effects on emotional and cognitive development, see Siegel (2003) and van der Kolk (2003).

A second aspect of sexual trauma is emotional isolation. Traumatized youth sense that they are "different" from their peers when they realize that their own sexual experiences do not reflect the related experiences of other kids their age. In addition, victims of sexual abuse or shame are often pressured either directly or indirectly to maintain secrecy to protect the public images of their families or perpetrators. This experience of "difference" may remain hidden as an aspect of self-perception or it may be acted out in the victims' social interactions, leading to further isolation. As an example, one young gay man described to a researcher this aspect of sexual trauma arising out of homophobic sexual shame he experienced in a Catholic high school:

> In one of the interview questions, I asked Mark what elements in his high school he would have called "safe." His answer was very disturbing. "Safe? That's a really weird word for a Catholic high school. I don't think there was anything safe. I mean, the only security I got was to hear that bell ring for us to leave. Even then, the bus ride to my car wasn't safe." He continued with this theme later in the interview. "Almost everything was unsafe to me, especially in high school. It was small, and so there really wasn't any place to go. It was very risky. Everyone was very unsafe to me; I had few friends. To me, it was like I was out in the wilderness. I was out in a jungle, and I had to fend for myself." (Maher, 2001, p. 33)

The cumulative experience of unattended sexual trauma for developing youth inevitably results in a reduced sense of personal power and control in their interpersonal relationships. They may accept this sense of powerlessness as fact and resolve themselves to passivity and dependence, or they may use their relationships as opportunities to test their power and capacity for control. Either way, these youth become vulnerable to exploitation, revictimization, and further difficulties through interpersonal submissiveness on the one hand or high-risk social and sexual behavior on the other.

Effects on Childhood and Adolescence

Studies support that roughly 60 to 80 percent of children who are sexually traumatized through direct sexual abuse develop significant symptoms within the first 18 months of the traumatic event, regardless of family environment and abuse-related variables (Putnam, 2003). There is some evidence to suggest that these symptoms may initially appear as a result of neuropsychological disturbance during critical periods of brain development either in early childhood or early adolescence (Schore, 2003). With exposure to overwhelming and chronic stress, excessive cortisol secretions may kill neuronal cells and damage neural circuitry development, particularly in the hippocampus (Siegel, 2003). Most often, children and adolescents who were traumatized through sexual abuse express symptoms of post-traumatic stress including depression, social withdrawal, anxiety, flashbacks, dissociation, nightmares, and hyperarousal. In addition, behavior problems often arise, including aggression and sexualized behaviors. Traumatized boys often present more obvious and extreme behavioral symptoms than girls (Gartner, 1999; Putnam, 2003). Though specific effects of sexual trauma resulting from interpersonal transactions other than direct sexual abuse have not yet been studied, there is reason to believe that, with sufficient trauma, the effects may be similar.

Research is still inconclusive as to the longer term outcomes for abused children who initially present with minimal or no significant symptoms. It may be that with a supportive environment some abused children continue to grow and develop symptom-free. Others may have coping styles that mask symptoms that will eventually manifest in later adolescence or adulthood. However, studies of nonclinical samples suggest that the majority of sexually abused children qualify for at least one psychiatric disorder whether they receive treatment or not (Putnam, 2003).

In adolescence, the consequences of sexual trauma may become more severe with increased social pressure, independence from the family, and exposure to alcohol and drugs. Studies indicate that adolescents with a history of maltreatment, including physical abuse, sexual abuse, or neglect, are more likely to experience anxiety, depressive symptoms, suicidal ideation, teenage pregnancy, substance abuse, aggression or other antisocial behavior, homelessness, and juvenile detention than adolescents with no history of reported maltreatment (Cauce, Tyler, and Whitbeck, 2004; Kimball and Golding, 2004; Smith, Thornberry and Ireland, 2004). These outcomes appear to be just as likely whether adolescents are exposed to maltreatment from the time of childhood or they experience maltreatment for the first time in adolescence (Smith, Thornberry, and Ireland, 2004).

In the context of the family system, there are circular relationships between causes and effects of sexual trauma. Parental neglect of the emotional needs of children may serve as a primary risk factor for sexual abuse. Likewise, the manner and timing of abuse disclosure, the nature of the family's response, and the resulting level of trauma experienced by the child or adolescent may either be mediated or complicated by a number of family characteristics. The behavioral effects of sexual trauma expressed by the child or adolescent affect participation in the family system. Undetected trauma of a child or adolescent member may result in the evolution or exacerbation of additional family dysfunction as well as individual problems for other members. For example, in some families in which an older child has been sexually traumatized, that child may become sexually or physically abusive to younger siblings.

What Facilitates Early Recovery?

The first necessary component of recovery from early childhood sexual abuse is detection by victims' parents that abuse has occurred and that they make certain the abuse is ended. For sexually coercive abuse during adolescence, it is especially critical that the victims themselves recognize that these relationships were sexually exploitative. In either case, victims must come to realize that the abusive encounters were of no fault of their own. For those traumatized through sexual shame, the sources of shame most often originate with the parents, intensifying the effects of emotional isolation. In order for these victims to recognize that they were not deserving of the maltreatment, they must have access to normalizing positive role models, such as teachers or other authority figures with whom they can discuss their areas of conflict.

Second, sexually traumatized children and adolescents must have strong, secure emotional attachments to a responsive parent or significant caregiver to re-establish interpersonal safety and to correct negative perceptions of self and others. In some cases, victims may also need assistance with grieving the loss of the nurturing aspects of their relationships with the perpetrators. Ideally, this corrective process occurs immediately after the traumatizing episode is discovered so as to minimize secondary trauma associated with behavioral problems that may arise before the initial trauma can be addressed. Friedrich (1990), who has worked with and written extensively on sexually abused children and their families, emphasizes that sexually reactive behavior in traumatized children and youth should be managed by using positive reinforcement techniques for nonreactive behaviors and disciplining strategies that are free from guilt-laden or sexually shaming overtones. It is critical that traumatized children and adolescents are given as much personal freedom and control over their lives as is safe and age-appropriate. Needless to say, the parenting styles and overall family functioning in the home environments of recovering youth have a tremendous impact on the outcomes of sexual trauma.

Early recovery from sexual trauma also seems to be assisted by the personal strengths of victims that may offer resources for building self-esteem and enhancing peer relationships. Athletic abilities, strong academic aptitude, and artistic talents are good examples of personal attributes that may allow traumatized youth opportunities to re-establish a sense of personal power, receive appropriate positive attention from adults, and build healthy social networks with peers.

Prendergast (1993, p. 109) summarizes the process of recovery in treatment for adult survivors of sexual trauma as consisting of ten steps that can be facilitated through a therapeutic relationship:

1. Return control or responsibility to the survivor
2. Ventilate the anger fully
3. Full disclosure of the abuse or attack
4. Ventilate all associated feelings
5. New image formation [beyond victim persona]

6. Value reassessment
7. Begin [positive] risk-taking behaviors
8. Progressive but rapid promotion [of independence in therapy]
9. Reality orientation to new life
10. Provision for follow-up (PRN-termination)

Those Who Do Not Survive to Adulthood

Tragically, suicide and other sources of premature death claim the lives of many sexually traumatized youth before they have time to access help. Suicide is the third leading cause of death among young people between the ages of fifteen and twenty-four years, following unintentional injuries and homicide (NIMH, 2004). While the specific reasons for these suicides are almost impossible to ascertain after the fact, we know from studies of adolescents who have experienced sexual abuse that they are significantly more likely to seriously consider or attempt suicide than adolescents who have not experienced sexual abuse (Kimball and Golding, 2004).

Research also indicates that the risk of suicide attempts may be twice as high for high school students who report having same-sex sexual contact as compared to those who report having other-sex sexual contact (Faulkner and Cranston, 1998). Likewise, in a study of self-identified gay, lesbian, and bisexual youth, 40 percent reported having attempted suicide and another 26 percent reported seriously considering suicide. Those who had poor family relationships, lacked social support, and had negative self-perceptions were assessed at the greatest risk for committing suicide (Proctor and Groze, 1994).

Many sexually traumatized youth also may attempt to manage their overwhelming feelings by engaging in high-risk behaviors such as running away from home, abusing alcohol and drugs, becoming sexually promiscuous, or participating in various criminal activities (Kimball and Golding, 2004). The results too often include homelessness, chemical addiction, HIV, or other serious illness, incarceration, accidental death, or homicide before these youngsters ever have a chance to recover or otherwise lead happy and fulfilling lives.

Long-Term Effects of Unresolved Sexual Trauma

The common effects of unresolved sexual trauma fall within a cluster of symptoms that mental health researchers describe as disorders of extreme stress not otherwise specified (DESNOS). Extreme stress may result from any traumatic event experienced throughout the lifecycle with the following effects:

1. Altered affect regulation such as persistent dysphoria, chronic suicidal preoccupation, and explosive or inhibited anger [commonly experienced as feeling depressed all the time, "moody," irritable, or "hot tempered"]
2. Transient alterations of consciousness, such as flashbacks and dissociative episodes [intrusive memories of the trauma and/or experiences of mentally "checking out" in situations perceived to be threatening]
3. Altered self-perceptions including helplessness, shame, guilt, and self-blame [very low self-esteem]
4. Altered relationships with others, such as persistent distrust, withdrawal, failures of self-protection, and rescuer fantasies [often experienced by companions as tentativeness or unpredictable "pushing and pulling" in the relationship]
5. Altered systems of meanings, including loss of sustaining faith, hopelessness, and despair [feeling lost or without purpose in the world]
6. Somatization [physical manifestations of illness, pain, nausea, hyper-arousal, etc.] (Herman, 1992, as cited in Putnam, 2003, p. 274. Comments in brackets were added by author.)

In my experience of working with adults who were sexually traumatized in childhood or adolescence, I have noticed that the most pervasive and persistent effects are issues related to personal power and control. Every interpersonal exchange is filtered as a potential challenge to one's autonomy or safety, triggering an automatic "fight-or-flight" response to situations perceived as threatening. Individuals may struggle almost constantly either to restore some sense of personal power that was lost during the trauma or to minimize feelings of powerlessness in relation to the social environment. Some become masters at predicting and controlling their social surroundings, often appearing as aggressive leaders among their peers. Others develop sophisticated strategies to avoid interpersonal conflict so they do not risk feeling overwhelmed and powerless. Ironically, this avoidance of conflict can lead many to simply divert authority to an external source of control, seeking respite in dependency. Adults with unresolved childhood sexual trauma tend to rest at one end of the spectrum or the other most of the time as either interpersonally aggressive or overly compliant, but they may alternate under certain conditions or when triggered by unexpected flashbacks to the traumatic episode.

Those who tend toward interpersonal aggression rely on cognitive distortions or denial to manage unwelcome feelings of empathy for others they may hurt or oppress. Those who tend toward passive compliance rely on dissociation in situations where they are not otherwise in control. Both denial and dissociation accomplish the same effect of removing a person's cognitive awareness from his or her physical behavior or emotional experience. In my estimation, these two psychological defenses are closely related. When either of these two default modes fails to be strong enough to ward off painful emotions or memories, traumatized individuals may eventually turn to substance abuse or other compulsive behaviors to temporarily sever the mental bridges between physical sensation, thoughts, and emotion.

Compulsive behaviors can also offer a temporary sense of power and control for adults with unresolved sexual trauma during times of personal vulnerability or stress. These behaviors can include substance abuse, eating disorders, compulsive sex, gambling, competitive sports, compulsive exercise, perfectionism, etc. For those who engage in compulsive sex, they may consciously or unconsciously play out the dynamics of their childhood traumas in a way that allows them to experience the role of the perpetrator. Especially for traumatized men, this compulsion may take the form of recurrent aggressive pursuits of multiple sexual partners. Women, on the other hand, more often use the culturally accessible roles of manipulative seduction to secure a position of power and control in interpersonal sexual dynamics. If these compulsive patterns become so pervasive that they become the primary focus of an individual's life, then the behavior may be referred to as a "sexual addiction" (Carnes, 1991).

Sexually traumatized individuals who rely more on avoidance to manage feelings of powerlessness may tend to abstain from sexual contact altogether. In order to justify their sexual withdrawal, while also restoring a sense of personal power, they may focus on the flaws of their potential partners as an excuse to remain sexually unavailable. For some, this psychological defense evolves into rigid sexual intolerance and condemnation of others. Religious-based moral judgments about sexuality are conveniently employed by many traumatized adults who cannot face their overwhelming fears of sexual vulnerability.

Yet, a third scenario is that of the sexually traumatized adult who is passive and dependent in most adult relationships, but finds opportunity to feel powerful in relation to children or to specific adults whom they see as nonthreatening. These individuals rely on positions of status within their own families or a secure and isolated social system that shelters them from the unpredictable challenges of the greater social environment. I refer to this pattern as one of *incestuous narcissism.* Research studies on incestuous fathers report that these men most often present as passive and dependent among peers and in psychological testing, yet many also have histories of domestic violence or tyrannical control within their own households (Cole, 1992; Williams and Finkelhor, 1990). Likewise, it appears that most female sex offenders of children "tend to be low-status members of their peer groups and feel that they do not belong anywhere. They are often friendless and willing to do almost anything for acceptance" (Matthews, 1994, p. 58). During times of stress and/or limited emotional resources, these individuals may seek immediate relief from personal distress or loneliness through isolated or episodic sexual encounters with those who are most vulnerable to them. This pattern may also apply to professionals described as "regressed" or "lovesick" offenders who sexually exploit their clients in order to meet their own narcissistic needs for validation and interpersonal power (Gabbard, 1995; Gonsiorek, 1995). Based on available research and anecdotal evidence, it seems that the majority of priests and nuns who sexually exploit youth and vulnerable adults also fall into this category (Markham and Mikail, 2004).

Illustration of the Cycle of Sexual Trauma

A continuum of possible outcomes of childhood sexual trauma is schematically presented in Figure 5.2. As discussed in the preseding sections, this diagram illustrates how both childhood sexual abuse and childhood sexual shame may contribute to a cycle of sexual trauma. Through the experience of sexual trauma, a child loses his or her sense of personal power and control. The effects of trauma may be mediated or exacerbated by the family environment and individual

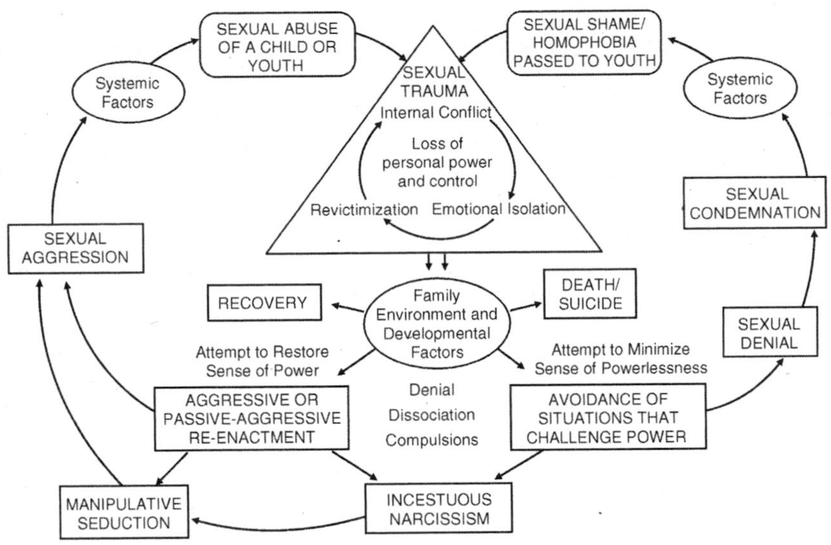

FIGURE 5.2. The Cycle of Sexual Trauma

developmental factors that either strengthen or weaken the child's coping strategies. The outcomes of sexual trauma include resilient or therapeutic recovery at one end of the spectrum, and death or suicide at the other. For those whose traumatic experiences remain unresolved, social behavior becomes dictated by attempts to either restore feelings of power and control or to avoid feelings of powerlessness. Each of these dysfunctional coping styles can lead to maladaptive social behavior including patterns of aggressive dominance in interpersonal transactions, persistent passive submission in relationships, or controlled situations of incestuous narcissism. For some individuals, unacknowledged sexual trauma can lead to sexual compulsion as a way to regain a sense of power, either through aggressive sexual behavior or through manipulative seduction. On the other hand, some may rely on sexual denial as a means of avoiding anxiety, or sexual condemnation as an attempt to control sexual arousal. Depending on individual, situational, and systemic factors, these coping strategies may result in the sexual neglect, abuse, or traumatic shaming of a vulnerable child or youth, feeding a cycle of sexual trauma.

RISK FACTORS FOR SEXUAL OFFENDING BY PRIESTS AND NUNS

The questions still remain of why sexual offending against minors may be more prevalent among Catholic priests and nuns than it is among men and women in other areas of society, and why priests and nuns more often abuse youth of their same gender. My hypothesis is that priests and nuns, as a subpopulation of devoutly religious Catholics, were more likely as youth to have been exposed to sexual trauma through sexually shameful beliefs, especially regarding both female sexual expression and homosexuality, than other men and women in society. Second, for those who were sexually traumatized as youth, their levels of trauma were more likely to have been severe and less likely to be adequately addressed before entering the seminary or convent. Third, the higher prevalence of severe, unresolved sexual trauma among priests and nuns as a group, combined with the four factors of sexual abuse perpetration, has put priests and nuns at higher risk for sexually offending in general, but especially for offending against pubescent and postpubescent youth of their same gender. I will discuss each of these factors in greater detail in the following sections.

Sexual Trauma

Several researchers have explored the possibility that nuns and priests may have a higher prevalence of childhood sexual abuse histories as a means of explaining both initial attraction to a celibate lifestyle and a higher risk for sexual offending. However, Chibnall, Wolf, and Duckro (1998) found that nuns report a similar prevalence of childhood sexual abuse as other women in the general population. Likewise, studies of cleric sex offenders have not found priest offenders to have higher rates of childhood sexual abuse than what we would expect to find among other male sex offenders or men in general (John Jay College, 2004; Haywood, Kravitz, Wasyliw et al., 1996; Langevin, Curnoe, and Bain, 2000). However, it may be that, despite having equal or lower prevalence of direct childhood sexual *abuse* as other populations, nuns and priests have a higher prevalence of childhood sexual *trauma*.

For those who were sexually abused in childhood, it is likely that their abuse was never disclosed or addressed in a way that promoted early recovery. Steward and Driskill (1991) conducted a study of devoutly religious Christian families and their churches regarding attitudes toward child abuse, and concluded that victims of childhood sexual abuse in religious families may be less inclined to disclose the abuse because of sexual shame and authoritarian parenting styles often promoted by conservative theological beliefs. In addition, we know from the John Jay College (2004) study of priest offenders and the Chibnall, Wolf, and Duckro (1998) study of nuns that those who were victims of childhood sexual abuse were more likely to have been abused by Catholic religious offenders than childhood victims from the general population. Assuming that these victims, who later became priests and nuns, are much like others victims of childhood sexual abuse by priests, nuns, or other religious leaders, it is likely that they carried with them severe, religious-based sexual trauma that was never adequately addressed until much later in adulthood.

It is also likely that much of the sexual trauma experienced by priests and nuns in childhood came more from chronic sexual shame than from direct sexual abuse, especially in the form of sexual beliefs that were discordant with their own erotic feelings and experiences. As children and youth, themselves, growing up in Catholic families, it is reasonable to assume that many future priests and nuns experienced fear of humiliation or harsh punishment for any interest they may have shown in sexual gratification, particularly if it was homosexual in nature. The "unhealed wound," as Eugene Kennedy (2002) describes it, may begin as a minor injury in childhood that is repeatedly infected throughout development in every moment of erotic sensation that is experienced as shameful and alienating.

The internal means of coping over time with unresolved sexual trauma resulting from chronic sexual shame seems to be very similar to what often happens as a result of direct sexual abuse. The child manages psychologically discordant experiences by disconnecting cognitive beliefs from physical sensation and emotion. Though the visible signs of trauma resulting from chronic sexual shame may be less obvious than the initial signs of sexual abuse, the internal experience of trauma over time may evolve to be essentially the same.

In my experience, this is particularly applicable to sexual trauma arising from religious-based homophobia. Michael Maher (2001) conducted a qualitative study of the experiences of young gay men and lesbians who attended Catholic high schools in the 1990s. He found that most of them experienced some degree of chronic stress during adolescence, resulting in poor self-esteem, depression, anxiety, social withdrawal, and other symptoms of trauma, even for those who did not yet recognize their sexual orientations. In addition, most resorted to using repression or denial of sexuality in a process that Maher describes as "dis-integration" of the sexual aspects of themselves from every other aspect of life. The realms of "dis-integration" that Maher studied included family life, socialization, institutional involvement, spirituality, and identity development.

What I find to be particularly interesting is that research on child sexual abuse and religion suggests that poorly integrated, conservative religious beliefs may contribute to higher rates of sexual offending than well integrated or more liberal religious beliefs (Elliott, D. M., 1994; Gebhard et al., 1965; Price, 1995; Saradjian and Nobus, 2003). In one study by Haywood and associates, they found that, like other child molesters, priest offenders are significantly more likely to profess conservative sexual values. In addition, they found that priest offenders report having significantly lower sex drive and fewer heterosexual experiences than either nonoffenders or other child molesters (Haywood, Kravitz, Grossman et al., 1996). Greeley (2004) reported findings from a 2002 survey of priests, which indicated that new, less experienced priests are much more conservative in theological beliefs and sexual values than are older, more experienced priests. All of these findings, combined with what we know about the effects of unresolved sexual trauma, particularly as it may apply to youth with "dis-integrated" homosexual experiences, support my hypothesis that, as a group, priests and nuns who molest postpubescent youth of the same gender may suffer from higher levels of homophobic sexual trauma than other populations of sex offenders.

Emotional Congruence with Pubescent and Postpubescent Youth

The factor of emotional congruence with children in Araji and Finkelhor's four-factor model of child sexual abuse (1986) lead us to question why some priests and nuns may feel more emotionally comfortable with youth rather than with their adult peers. Developmental theories suggest that unresolved childhood traumas can cause some adults to remain arrested in certain aspects of their psychosocial development. Offenders often relate to children of the same gender and the age that they were when they experienced their own childhood traumas. They are attracted to them as representatives of themselves at a point in their lives when they needed special care. Priest or nun offenders may initially approach their victims with the intention of offering them the nurturance and reassurance that they themselves craved when they were of the same age and in a similarly perceived social situation.

However, there is also buried anger and resentment that offenders may harbor for the children they once were, the inner children of the past who are now responsible for their current emotional insecurities. Indeed, psychological testing of priests who abused youth indicates that these men generally score higher than other sex offenders on measures of over-controlled hostility (Plante et al., 1996) and sexual conflictedness (Haywood, Kravitz, Wasyliw et al., 1996) and are more sexually/emotionally underdeveloped than other child molesters (Falkenhain et al., 1999). Thus, perpetrators' conflicted feelings about their own sexual development become projected onto their victims. While they may feel less threatened by youth, they may also grow to resent their dependency or other attributes of the youth that remind them of themselves.

We now know both anecdotally and empirically that a higher percentage of priests (Cozzens, 2002; Greeley, 2004), and possibly nuns (Curb and Manahan, 1985), identify themselves as homosexual than what we would expect to find in the general population. Gay and lesbian religious who have come to terms with their sexual orientations and can readily identify themselves as either homosexual or bisexual on surveys or in interviews may be the least likely to sexually abuse youth, as research suggests (Abel and Harlow, 2001; Jenny, Roesler, and Poyer, 1994; Rossetti, 1996, 2002). Loftus and Camargo (1993) found that priests in treatment who reported sexual activity with other men had significantly different personality profiles than priests who admitted to sexual activity with male youth. Those priests and nuns who have not integrated their sexual orientations as a part of their personal identities due to sexual shame may be at greater risk for unresolved sexual trauma and, therefore, also at greater risk for sexual offending. It is my belief that these unidentified, sexually conflicted priests and nuns may be at highest risk for sexually abusive or compulsive behavior with youth of the same gender and of the same age as when they experienced their own traumatic, experiences: during and just after puberty.

In addition, I have come to suspect from the stories of other survivors who have shared their experiences with me that a disproportionate number of victims of childhood sexual abuse by priests and nuns are themselves gay, lesbian, or bisexual in adulthood. Researchers who have observed this same phenomenon among adult male and female survivors of childhood sexual abuse in general have proposed two possible explanations: either the homosexual nature of their abuse led to the development of a homosexual orientation in adulthood, or youth inclined toward homosexual orientations may be at greater risk for being sexually abused than their heterosexual peers (Gebhard et al., 1965; Hislop, 2001). Based on my personal and professional experience in working with gay and lesbian survivors of childhood sexual abuse, I feel fairly confident that the latter of these two propositions applies to most cases of postpubescent sexual abuse. Sexual conflictedness in the developing youth, no matter what his or her orientation may be, is sensed and exploited by the adult perpetrator.

Other characteristics that have been associated with sexual offenders' emotional attraction to youth are their narcissistic needs to feel appreciated and relatively powerful, in control, or dominant. These needs may originate in the perpetrators' childhoods or they may be situationally triggered in times of stress, or both (Finkelhor, 1986; Markham and Mikail, 2004; Prendergast, 2004; Rossetti, 1996; Ward, Hudson and McCormack, 1997). With extra attention from an authority figure, most kids will readily gratify these narcissistic needs for their potential offenders, especially if their offenders are respected religious leaders and if the youth are already lacking in positive emotional attachments to caregivers (Finkelhor, 1986; Putnam, 2003).

Sexual Arousal Toward Target Victims

One major contributor of adult sexual arousal toward age-inappropriate sex objects is thought to be early learning experiences that reinforce and condition deviant erotic pleasure with abusive scenarios. Classical conditioning in which early sexual experiences are repeatedly or traumatically paired with negative situations may serve to link sexual gratification with intense emotional responses such as fear, anger, guilt, or shame. Likewise, operant conditioning of deviant sexual arousal patterns may also result from situations in which youth repeatedly reach sexual climax as a powerful reinforcement during forced or coerced sexual dynamics. Through this process, subsequent sexual arousal may become dependent upon the replication of the abusive sexual dynamics (Laws and Marshall, 1990; Schwartz, 1995). Once again, having a history of sexual trauma during childhood or adolescence may predispose future priests and nuns to deviant sexual arousal patterns in adulthood.

Among clergy sex offenders, deviant arousal patterns have been observed to be less extreme than those of nonclergy sex offenders but consistently present nonetheless (Langevin, Curnoe, and Bain, 2000). Since arousal patterns are measured using phallometric testing of the penis during exposure to sexually provocative stimuli, the test is only applicable for use with males. Since very little research has been done on female sexual arousal in general, there is little to compare with female sex offenders. Thus, we have no way of knowing if deviant sexual arousal may contribute to female offending in the same way that it does for male offending.

Neuropsychological disorders may also contribute to sexual arousal to age-inappropriate stimuli. For both cleric and noncleric child molesters, higher incidences of brain damage and dysfunction, particularly in the frontal and left temporal cortical regions, have been repeatedly found to correlate with sexual disorders and abusive behaviors (Carmago, 1997, as cited in John Jay College, 2004; Langevin, 1990; Lothstein, 1999). Deficits in the fronto-temporal areas of the brain are usually associated with poor judgment, impulsivity, and disinhibition. The specific areas of brain dysfunction among coercive child molesters also appear to be unique from the areas of dysfunction found among sadistic and aggressive sexual assaulters (Langevin, 1990). Historically, damage to the frontal and temporal regions of the brain has been linked to a history of serious head injuries or to excessive and prolonged alcohol or other chemical abuse. However, in an extensive study of sexually disordered, primarily Catholic clerics in treatment at The Institute for Living, the same patterns of neuropsychological deficits found in priest offenders could not be explained by either substance abuse or head injuries (Lothstein, 1999). Likewise, sex-offending priests with this type of neuropsychological dysfunction do not demonstrate the level of disorganization and antisocial pathology that is usually associated with such neurological damage.

Besides sexual impulsivity and neuropsychological abnormalities, the clerics in The Institute for Living study also shared common characteristics in psychiatric diagnoses and histories of childhood trauma. Along with diagnoses of various psychosexual disorders, the group also had a high prevalence of comorbid dysthymia (chronic, mild depression). In addition, most were first-born children in their families and reported histories of childhood sexual abuse (29 percent), physical abuse (56 percent), or other traumatic experience related to separations, abandonment, moves, and deaths (35 percent). Seventy-six percent of the men also presented fair to poor interpersonal relationship skills. These findings again suggest the possibility of a cycle of sexual trauma. As Leslie Lothstein, the Director of Psychology at The Institute for Living, points out in this study, "One may argue that the clergymen's familial and environmental chaos influenced their subsequent brain development and put them at risk for focal brain abnormality around limbic excitation" (1999, pp. 76-77).

Blockage in Adult Intimacy

Although priest sex offenders have been repeatedly found to have lower levels of psychiatric disturbance and antisocial personality traits than other offenders of minors, they also demonstrate higher levels of sexual conflictedness than other offenders (Haywood, Kravitz, Wasyliw et al., 1996). Likewise, as a group, priest perpetrators suffer fair to poor interpersonal relationship skills (Gerard, Jobes and Cimbolic, 2003; Lothstein, 1999). These intimacy deficits most likely reflect childhood emotional neglect or maltreatment from parents or significant caregivers. For future priests and nuns growing up in typically large Catholic families of the twentieth century, relational skill development and self-esteem may have suffered in families with limited resources in which parents were simply stretched too thin to adequately meet the emotional and social developmental needs of every child. Thus, childhood emotional neglect may account for a higher rate of intimacy deficits among some individuals entering the priesthood or convent from traditional Catholic families. It is also reasonable to expect that, for some who pursue religious life in community, this externally legitimized way of life may reflect an interior drive to recreate a nurturing family environment while avoiding the challenges of adult intimacy due to preexisting psychological factors.

While screening techniques may root out blatant psychological and/or sexual disorders in such individuals, they are less likely to detect subtle deficits in interpersonal intimacy skills in otherwise highly functional people. These interpersonal deficits may become intensified by social or emotional isolation once new priests and nuns complete their formation and assume positions in the larger community. With the additional pressure and scrutiny imposed by vows of celibacy or chastity, priests and nuns with compromised relationship skills may become more and more emotionally isolated with every new assignment to a different location, especially in small diocesan parishes. This issue perhaps partially explains the higher prevalence of child sexual offending by diocesan priests compared to religious order priests and nuns who more often live in community environments. It may also help to explain why priest and nun offenders who may be heterosexual or sexually indifferent in orientation abuse victims of their same gender as a simple factor of access. While they may be socially and emotionally isolated from other adults, ministry settings often offer priests and nuns disproportionate access to same-sex youth through gender-specific youth programs and single-sex schools, where intimate bonding is allowed to develop.

Disinhibition

According to Finkelhor (1984), potential child molesters must ultimately overcome both internal and external sources of inhibition in order to indulge their impulses to the point of committing criminal offenses. For priests and nuns in the Catholic Church, there are unique issues that may affect how potential child molesters can overcome normal inhibitions before carrying out their abusive acts. Internal inhibitions are regulated by individual characteristics such as capacities for empathy and impulse control, ethical values and beliefs, and cognitive processes. Despite undergoing rigorous training and practiced discipline regarding moral beliefs, priests and nuns who have limited or distorted sexual experience may have greater difficulty recognizing sexual cues that would normally trigger cognitive inhibitions.

Some religious sex offenders manage to twist their moral and theological beliefs into excuses and justifications for their sexually abusive behavior. In a qualitative study on the cognitive distortions of religious professionals who sexually abuse children, Saradjian and Nobus (2003) found that these offenders often use their religious roles and perceived relationships with God within their distorted beliefs to minimize internal inhibitions before and after offending. These beliefs were specifically noted in the areas of giving themselves permission to offend as something they deserve after working so hard, denying the likelihood of getting caught because of their privileged status, reducing their feelings of guilt based on God's acceptance and forgiveness of them, and maintaining a positive self-image as special caregivers for their victims.

In the realm of external sources of inhibition, systemic factors play the most important role in either protecting children and potential offenders from dangerous situations or putting them both at greater risk for abusive encounters. That priests and nuns were so often granted unquestionable and privileged access to children by Catholic parents may have allowed potential offenders to disregard any sense of accountability owed to them. In addition, the lax, forgiving, and often protective responses of bishops and religious leaders to priests and nuns accused of sexually abusing children has facilitated an environment in which the usual cultural taboos against sexual behavior with minors have been diminished. Researchers comparing clergy offenders to nonclergy offenders have repeatedly found that clergy offenders are significantly less likely to face criminal charges than nonclergy offenders of similar social status, even when they commit more serious crimes (Langevin, Curnoe, and Bain, 2000; Bottoms et al., 1995). This factor would certainly account for the extremely high number of victims for the most notorious, though few, compulsive priest offenders who were transferred from parish to parish. Every sexually gratifying transgression that does not result in negative consequences serves as a powerful reinforcement for repeating the behavior with less and less inhibition.

On the other side of the equation are the characteristics of Catholic children that make them less resistant to sexual advances by religious professionals. Because priests and nuns are held in the highest esteem in Catholic culture, higher even than their own parents, children are made that much more vulnerable to abuse and trauma by the nature of the power differential. In addition, traditionally large Catholic families with many children close in age often have to rely on and trust community resources to assist with supervision and child care, increasing the chances for abuse outside the home. Likewise, Catholic children who have poor or inadequate relationships with their parents may be ill equipped to defend themselves psychologically against the initial grooming process and sexual advances of esteemed adults.

The resulting trauma experienced by Catholic youth abused by religious professionals may be more severe if there are preexisting attachment deficiencies in the victim's parental relationships. It is less likely that children who have insecure attachments with parents will be inclined to disclose the abuse, and it is perhaps less likely that they will be believed if they do tell a parent. In addition, devoutly Catholic parents may themselves become traumatized upon learning that their spiritual leaders betrayed them. These parents may react to the disclosure of their children's abuse from a victim's perspective rather than maintaining a protective, authoritative posture. In these cases, as in my own, parents may experience such extreme shame that they then resort to secrecy and silence themselves.

Chapter 6

Implications for Recovery, Research, and Prevention

As stated in the introduction to this book, my ultimate goal is to shift attention in the Catholic sexual abuse crisis to a need for healing dialogue, further research, and informed prevention strategies. Before systemic healing or effective prevention of sexual abuse can take place within the Church, the power struggles between various political factions and individuals with self-serving interests related to this crisis must end. Whether the feuding is fueled by sincere efforts to promote positive change, by naïve hopes that the problem has already been solved, or by narcissistic opportunism to exert vengeance, it is not effective in addressing the primary source of dysfunction, namely, the sexual shaming and abuse of untold numbers of faithful Catholics over centuries of church history. This includes those boys and girls who were emotionally and sexually neglected, shamefully maltreated, and sexually abused in their youth only to become the religious predators of the next generation. This chapter explores what I believe will be necessary to heal the wounded of the Catholic Church and to restructure the Church system into the functional spiritual family that perhaps the original Apostles intended it to be.

One hope I have held while writing this book is to bridge the gaps between various perspectives on the sexual abuse crisis in the Catholic Church so that an atmosphere of healing dialogue may be achieved. As a recovering victim of sexual abuse by a nun, an estranged Catholic, a psychotherapist, and a social worker, I can appreciate multiple perspectives and needs during this time of systemic turmoil. Victims

Sexual Abuse and the Culture of Catholicism

doi:10.1300/5633_06

of Catholic sexual abuse and exploitation need immediate validation, sincere apologies, and healing support from their families, spiritual leaders, and faith communities. They need the undisturbed space, respect, and freedom to work though their own anger and despair without others interfering to promote their own personal or political agendas. Likewise, the faithful laity, the children of the Church, need reassurance of compassionate, cooperative, and trustworthy leaders who can offer them both the richness and stability of tradition and the openness and flexibility to accommodate their evolving spiritual needs. And in order for the current leaders of the Catholic Church to resume their roles as spiritually responsible parents, they must be willing to participate in honest and humble communication with the laity and with each other to critically re-examine their shared functions and responsibilities as spiritual leaders, to realign systemic power structures in the Church, and to either work toward renewed passion and commitment between discordant leadership positions, or to respectfully agree to separate for the good of the entire church family.

HEALING THE WOUNDED

The wounded of the sexual abuse crisis in the Catholic Church are many. In need of immediate attention are those who were directly victimized by priests, brothers, deacons, nuns, and other lay religious professionals. They include children, adolescents, men, and women of all sexual orientations and at various levels of involvement within and outside of the Church system. Also among those who need specialized attention and treatment are the secondary victims of the crisis—victims' and perpetrators' families, communities of worship, and religious congregations. There are also the hidden wounded of the Church, the sexually traumatized among the faithful who were not directly abused by their religious leaders but have been chronically shamed for having erotic desires and intimate longings that do not match the Church's imposed restrictions on conjugal love. Finally, there are the wounded perpetrators—the priests, nuns, and other religious ministers whose individual injuries have been so tightly guarded that their layers of armor have rendered them dangerous.

Primary Victims

Before the primary victims of the crisis can begin to recover from the traumatic effects of sexual shame, abuse, and exploitation, they need safe opportunities to share with someone that they have been harmed. Although at least 10,505 of the juvenile victims of sexual abuse by priests and deacons have reported the offenses to church or civil authorities (John Jay College, 2004), it is likely that twice as many of their juvenile victims have never reported the abuses they suffered. According to the National Crime Victimization Survey, less than one-third of all sex crimes are ever reported to authorities (Greenfeld, 1997). In addition, there are uncounted numbers of adult victims of priests and deacons and both adult and juvenile victims of religious figures other than clergy who are yet to be collectively recognized in the official accounts of damage caused by the church's sexual abuse disaster.

Many different issues may affect victims' abilities or desires to disclose that they were sexually abused or exploited. Among the issues that have been identified in the professional literature as affecting disclosure by juvenile victims of abuse are the following issues as they were listed in the review for the John Jay College report (2004):

- *Victim's relationship to the perpetrator.* If the perpetrator is a relative or close acquaintance, the victim is less likely to report the offense or to report it only after significant delay. One study found that 73 percent of women sexually abused in childhood by a family relative, and 70 percent of those abused by an acquaintance, never reported the abuse.
- *Severity of the abuse.* Though research results vary on this issue, it has been suggested that less severe forms of contact sexual abuse, such as fondling, may be more likely to be reported to authorities than more severe or prolonged abuse, except among assaultive cases of child rape. Thus, some of the most severely affected victims of sexual abuse never identify themselves as such.
- *Developmental and cognitive variables.* Younger children who are sexually abused may be more likely to tell about their abuse during childhood, while older victims are more likely to worry

about the social consequences of disclosure and therefore wait until adulthood to disclose if ever.

- *Fear of negative consequences.* If children have been threatened with further harm by their perpetrators, they are less likely to tell someone about it during childhood. However, some studies have suggested that the level of guilt and shame experienced by victims is what prevents many from disclosing the abuse to a parent or other authority figure.
- *Gender differences.* In general, it appears that girls are more likely to disclose sexual abuse than boys are. However, this seems to be a less critical issue affecting disclosure than the nature of the victim's relationship to the perpetrator.

In my own experience and in working with other victims or survivors of childhood sexual abuse, I have recognized more specific factors that may influence disclosure of abuse to family members or appropriate authorities. In regard to the victim's relationship to the perpetrator, familial relatedness seems to be an especially potent deterrent to disclosure if the perpetrator holds privileged status in the victim's family. Often, adult children who were sexually abused feel more secure in disclosing their history of abuse if their parents become separated or once the perpetrator or other influential relatives are deceased. This also seems to be a pattern for cases of abuse by religious leaders in which the perpetrator is a close friend or member of the victim's family.

Another issue that I think is particularly relevant to sexual abuse in the Catholic Church is the level of identification the victim may share with the perpetrator if they are both members of a marginalized or minority culture. For instance, if both the victim and the perpetrator are vowed religious, are both of the same ethnic minority group, are both affected by a physical disability, or are both homosexually oriented, the victim may feel especially conflicted about revealing the abuse. Despite having feelings of anger and disgust toward their offenders, they may either feel guilty or afraid of rejection by their minority community for "betraying" their culture by accusing a fellow member of such scandalous perversion. They may also fear being cast into the same light as their perpetrators by the dominant, majority culture. Unfortunately, these fears have proven valid for many gay and lesbian victims of same-sex abuse by priests and nuns.

Once victims of sexual abuse by priests or other religious professionals disclose their experiences to family and friends, they may or may not wish to report the offense to civil or church officials. This should always be a matter of choice for the individual. However, when an identified perpetrator is in a known situation to potentially abuse other children, anonymous reporting is advised for anyone who has suspicions of further abuse, and is legally mandated for health-care providers, educators, and human service professionals in most states. If the victim does choose to report the offense himself or herself, it should be the Church's first concern to offer immediate support while the details of the allegation are being investigated. Too often, victims of abuse in the Catholic Church have come forward only to be treated with disrespect and suspicion by religious leaders, ignoring the fact that they have before them a member of their faith who is in desperate need of spiritual affirmation, regardless of the particulars of their abuse allegations.

The therapeutic needs of people who were sexually abused or exploited by religious leaders are perhaps as diverse as the victims themselves. Certain elements of the therapeutic process, however, are essential. For severely traumatized individuals, a preliminary period of inpatient treatment may be needed to ensure safety and to assess for possible medication needs. Once safety is secured and there is no immediate crisis, most victims of sexual abuse require individual psychotherapy and perhaps family therapy to begin their healing journeys with a licensed mental health professional who is both compassionate and competent. For a victim to pursue counseling with anyone other than a licensed and experienced psychotherapist is to risk a recreation of the abusive scenario. In addition, the therapist chosen should be religiously neutral and practice meticulous professional boundaries in order to establish emotional safety in the therapeutic relationship. Consistent interpersonal boundaries and a well-contained professional relationship are critical if the therapy is to address the most painful and complex areas of personal injury.

Professionally sponsored Internet resources and issue-specific support groups can be very helpful as well, especially in the earlier phases of abuse disclosure when addressing emotional isolation and a need for normalization of the abuse survivor's experiences are the primary focus of concern. Support groups for sexual abuse survivors are usually offered to the public for free or for a nominal fee by nonprofit organizations, and can also be helpful in preparing individuals for more intensive work in therapy. However, support groups that are peer facilitated without professional supervision may struggle at times with maintaining group safety and equilibrium between participants. In addition, support groups can sometimes get "stuck" on a particular topic that has limited benefit to the overall healing process, and general membership participation may become irregular as a result.

Professionally facilitated group therapy can be especially helpful for clients once they have become emotionally stable. Many community-based counseling agencies and private mental health practitioners offer groups for survivors of various forms of abuse issues. I find that cofacilitated, professional therapy groups of diverse yet balanced client composition offer the richest healing potential for clients who have issues related to earlier childhood experiences or who are struggling with interpersonal relationships and trust issues. However, cofacilitated, mixed-gender and mixed-sexual-orientation groups usually require an extended time to establish group cohesion and membership stability. Thus, this variety of group therapy is less commonly offered than single-gender groups facilitated by an individual therapist.

Secondary Victims

The families of sexual abuse victims or adults who were sexually exploited often need time to adjust to the revelation that their loved ones were sexually, psychologically, spiritually, and sometimes physically harmed by religious professionals. The victim's parents may become overwhelmed with grief, anger, and guilt for having failed to protect their children from the abuse. Spouses and intimate partners of recently disclosed abuse victims or survivors will have their own reactions and concerns about how the disclosure and the effects of the abuse will impact their relationship and possibly their partners' relationships with their children. These issues and concerns are best handled by addressing them directly and honestly with the abuse survivor. Additional support from a family therapist can be a tremendous help when communication seems too difficult to manage without assistance.

Other secondary victims of sexual abuse and exploitation by religious leaders include the Church parishes, religious congregations, schools, ministry organizations of the perpetrator, and most often the victim of the abuse as well. Ideally, meetings should be held with the members of these various communities to disclose the abuse allegations accurately and fairly. Members should be encouraged to respectfully discuss their reactions and feelings openly with each other and, when appropriately invited, with either the victim or the perpetrator. Honest and heartfelt communication within affected communities is an important element of the healing process for everyone involved. Unfortunately, legal consultants often discourage open dialogue if there is any possibility of litigation. This is one area in which a legalistic approach functions counter to the healing needs of individuals who may already feel emotionally isolated, abandoned, or ashamed.

The Sexually Traumatized Faithful

As Helen Singer Kaplan (1974), author of the longstanding premier text on treating sexual dysfunctions, has stated:

> Unfortunately our society equates sex and sin. Therefore, every manifestation of a person's craving for sexual pleasure is apt to be denied, ignored or treated as a shameful thing and in general relentlessly assaulted with painful associations and consequences, especially during the critical childhood years. (p. 145)

Just as there is nothing inherently evil about being sexually aware and expressive, there is nothing particularly sacred or "pure" about being sexually naïve or avoidant. Yet this is not the message that we were taught to believe in Catholic homes and schools around the globe. Consequently, many Catholics struggle, often in shameful silence, with debilitating sexual disorders, which in turn can lead to interpersonal difficulties and intimacy deficits. For many of the couples I have worked with who were affected by sexual dysfunction, the topic of sexuality itself could often rouse so much anxiety in one or both partners that they would wind up fighting about something completely unrelated just to avoid the subject of sex. At the source of this anxiety are deep-seated feelings of shame and fears that their loved ones will either reject and abandon them or consume them out of a desperate attempt to restore a sense of power that was taken from them long ago.

Gay, lesbian, and bisexual (GLB) Catholics often experience extreme levels of sexual shame in the early stages of the "coming out" process. When they first begin to recognize their attractions as different from what is expected, many try to deny or change their orientations out of self-reproach. Even after outwardly accepting their sexuality and integrating it into their social identities, many continue to struggle with self-stigmatization based on the beliefs and attitudes upon which they were raised or on fears of being rejected by their families, friends, and faith communities. Such crippling levels of shame not only present problems for interpersonal relationships but can also create increased risks for substance abuse, compulsive disorders, and other self-destructive behaviors.

Whether in the context of an intimate relationship, family system, or faith community, having a loving, supportive, and nonjudgmental social network will grant the space and permission that these sexually wounded individuals need in order to heal. In addition, GLB youth and newly "out" adults need positive role models and a welcoming gay community that can provide them with a crucial sense of belonging. While members of other minority cultures have their own families with whom to fulfill this basic human need, GLB individuals must recreate a "gay family" in order to simulate the essential developmental tasks of healthy identity formation. This is why the existence of "gay subcultures" is so important. What is usually observed as immature or "campy" behavior in these subcultures is simply reflective of the developmental processes of individuals who are still in the earliest stages, or pubescence, of "coming out." The coming out process is normal, healthy, and progressive, just like adolescence is for everyone else. Within a nurturing environment, GLB individuals attain the same levels of adult functioning in their interpersonal relationships as their heterosexual peers. Ultimately, we must all be able to see ourselves as belonging to the beauty of "creation" in order to feel whole, happy, and spiritually alive. We all deserve to participate fully in the lives we were granted, each with our own unique ways of seeking meaning and purpose in the world around us.

Perpetrators

Like all sex offenders, religious professionals who use their positions of trust and authority to sexually exploit, coerce, or assault children and/or vulnerable adults need to be held fully responsible for their abusive behaviors, no matter what personal or situational factors may have contributed to their offenses. Likewise, they need to be removed and withheld from situations that may put them and any potential victims at risk for future offenses. However, not all perpetrators share the same motivations for offending or the same patterns of abusive behaviors, and therefore, it should not be assumed that all sex offenders should be treated alike. What is effective treatment for one may have disastrous results for another. Just as with victims of abuse, each individual perpetrator requires specialized evaluations and treatment planning tailored to their specific needs and to the safety needs of the public. Shame and isolation of sexual abusers can often put them at increased risk for repeating their offensive behavior patterns. In my opinion, priests and nuns who have been credibly accused of sexual violations should therefore remain under close supervision by either their superiors or, when offenses are criminal, by state correctional officers.

Some religious perpetrators are capable of demonstrating genuine empathy for their victims and taking full responsibility for their abusive behavior and its devastating effects once they have been through a successful treatment program. In these instances, it may be desirable for both the perpetrator and the victim to have an opportunity for a face-to-face, professionally facilitated meeting. Usually a single session is sufficient for victims to regain a cherished sense of personal power through directly confronting their offenders and revealing to them how the abuse has affected their lives. For remorseful perpetrators, these sessions may offer a critical opportunity to take personal responsibility and to apologize for the damages they caused. These meetings, when feasible to arrange, can have a tremendous influence on the course of healing for both individuals involved. In addition, healing in this area may contribute to the prevention of other potential problems for both.

The Church System

Throughout this book I have tried to explore every angle of the current crisis facing the Catholic Church with an open mind to the potential value offered by each perspective. In contrast to many conservatives in the Church, and even many liberals, I do not believe that the problems of the Church can be solved through simple, strategic, administrative steps to appease the anger of the laity, punish the crimes of the evil-doers, or suppress the sexual passions of the clergy. I see the problem of sexual abuse in the Catholic Church as an issue of systemic social dysfunction that has corrupted Catholicism over centuries through a cycle of systemic sexual trauma. The destructive effects are so pervasive that the problem of sexual abuse of children by priests and nuns is merely one symptom out of many that must be addressed.

Just as in the recovery process for incestuous families, the first step toward correcting this toxic cycle is for the Church's leaders—at every level of the hierarchical power structure—to take complete, defenseless ownership of their failures as the spiritual parents of the Church to protect the vulnerable laity in their care from the sexual predators among them. Church leaders, representing both the administrative and pastoral functions of the Church, must then be willing to participate in a restructuring of power, support, and communication between them through a process similar to marital therapy, but on a grand scale.

At the broadest level of the hierarchy, this would require priests, nuns, and lay ministers to take joint responsibility for the abuses that occurred under their watch and coordinate pastoral and administrative meetings so that all related leaders are present and involved in attending to the needs of the victims and perpetrators. Religious leaders who have shared responsibilities to the same faith communities must be willing to communicate openly, set mutually determined ministry goals based on the specific developmental needs of the faithful, and work together in a spirit of enthusiasm and support for each other. The imbalances of power between male and female leaders at the local and diocesan levels must be honestly explored and addressed based on the realities of talent, knowledge, experience, and skill. It is a disgrace to both genders to assume that male and female sources of authority and wisdom are neatly contained and mutually exclusive. Lastly, these religious professionals must take personal care and responsibility for their own social, psychological, and spiritual well-being through regular supervisory sessions, peer consultation, and balanced participation in appropriate activities and relationships outside of the Church environment.

At the highest levels of the Church hierarchy, fundamental issues regarding Catholic sexual theology and patriarchal authoritarianism must be re-examined in light of the sexual pathology they have created within the Church system. The failures of the early Christian fathers to fully grasp and appreciate the complex personal meanings and psychospiritual importance of human sexual experience must be accepted and placed appropriately into historical context along with other mistaken beliefs they had about the "nature of creation" that have been disproved at various times in church history. Likewise, the leadership style of the Catholic Church has changed very little since the Middle Ages despite the efforts of the Second Vatican Council in the early 1960s. This suggests that, in addition to simply prescribing a shift in attitudes toward the laity, there must be structural changes to ensure that the institutional church can return to a state of being the Church of the people as perhaps the first Apostles had envisioned.

The question remains, however, whether there is sufficient motivation and trust among the faithful of the Church to actively participate in the Church's recovery after such devastating betrayal within the current generation. If there is any hope, then immediate action must be taken to make radical adjustments in the leadership structures at the highest, most responsible levels. The time must come soon for a Vatican III if the institutional Catholic Church is to survive and function in a way that is attuned to the spiritual needs of both their pastoral partners and the faithful laity. If significant changes cannot be instated in the "marriage" between leaders as it stands, then it may also be time to consider a permanent separation to ensure the safety of the most vulnerable members of the family.

RESEARCH AND INFORMED PREVENTION

The church hierarchy must also be willing to work more openly with other resources in the global and local communities in order to provide responsible "parenting" to all its members, including sexual minority populations. Having a thorough understanding of the problem of sexual abuse is critical for prevention strategies to be effective, and the use of empirical research holds much more promise in gaining that understanding than reductionist theories based on political and theological conjecture. With evidence now indicating a higher prevalence of sexual offending with unique characteristics of abuse by Catholic clergy and other devout leaders of the faith, the festering sexual wounds of the Church can no longer be ignored. The treatment of this systemic infection must not simply rely on the superficial alleviation of obvious symptoms but on systemic interventions designed to specifically treat the source of the problem. Yet much more study is needed in order to pinpoint the most effective and feasible areas to target for leveraged intervention.

Based on the insights I have offered in this book, there is at least some possibility of reducing the prevalence of sexual offending by priests and nuns through the system-focused approaches described earlier and more targeted interventions aimed at reducing the individual risk factors for sexual offending by priests and nuns. Perhaps the future generations of the Church may be spared from the widespread devastation of sexual trauma that we have experienced today if the Church hierarchy becomes more open to the resources of science to assist them in making responsible decisions about policy. This would, however, require a dramatic shift in thinking on the part of our current papacy under the new Pope Benedict XVI.

Finally, the question must be addressed of what happens when religious systems within the broader social environment fail to function in the best interests of their members. If nothing changes within the Catholic Church and sexual abuse of children and vulnerable adults by priests and nuns continues at a level higher than in the general public, at what point do secular institutions have an ethical obligation to intervene without invitation? Maintaining the boundaries of separation of church and state must be a constant task that should include some measure of checks and balances. The sexual abuse scandal of 2002 revealed that all too often the Catholic Church was allowed to practice as though it was above the law of the land or above being evaluated by civil government. Meanwhile, religious groups in this country continue to wield powerful influence over civil government with unquestioned trust and authority, particularly as it affects our most vulnerable young citizens.

References

Abel, G. G., & Harlow, N. (2001). The Abel and Harlow child molestation prevention study. Excerpted from G. G. Abel, & N. Harlow, *The stop child molestation book.* Philadelphia: Xlibris Corporation. <stopchildmolestation.org>

Abel, G. G., & Rouleau, J. L. (1990).The nature and extent of sexual assault. In W. L. Marshall, D. R. Laws, & H. E. Barbaree (Eds.), *Handbook of sexual assault: Issues, theories, and treatment of the offender* (pp. 231-255). New York: Plenum Press.

Alexander, P. C. (1985). A systems theory conceptualization of incest. *Family Process, 24*, 79-88.

Allen, J. L. Jr. (2003a, April 18). Homosexuality a risk factor, Vatican told [Electronic version]. *National Catholic Reporter.* <natcath.org>

Allen, J. L. Jr. (2003b, August 25). Vatican official comments on Geoghan murder [Electronic version]. *National Catholic Reporter.* <natcath.org>

Aquinas, T. (1948). *Summa Theologica, 2-2, q. 154, art. 12.* (Fathers of the English Dominican Province, Trans.). New York: Benziger Brothers. (Original work published 1273).

Araji, S., & Finkelhor, D. (1986). *A sourcebook on child sexual abuse.* Beverly Hills: Sage Publications.

Bajt, T. R., & Pope, K. S. (1989). Therapist-patient sexual intimacy involving children and adolescents. *American Psychologist, 44,* 455.

Benedict, L. L., & Zautra, A. A. (1993). Family environmental characteristics as risk factors for childhood sexual abuse. *Journal of Clinical Child Psychiatry, 22,*3 65.

Berry, J. (1992). *Lead us not into temptation: Catholic priests and the sexual abuse of children.* New York: Doubleday.

Berry, J. (2002, April 3). Secrets, celibacy and the church. *The New York Times.* <nytimes.com>

Berry, J., & Renner, G. (2004). *Vows of Silence: The abuse of power in the papacy of John Paul II.* New York: Free Press.

Blackmon, R. A. (1984). *The hazards of the ministry.* Ann Arbor, MI: UMI Dissertation Services.

Bottoms, B. L., Shaver, P. R., Goodman, G. S., & Quin, J. (1995). In the name of God: A profile of religion-related child abuse. *Journal of Social Issues, 51,* 85-111.

Sexual Abuse and the Culture of Catholicism

doi:10.1300/5633_07

Brown, J. C. (1986). *Immodest acts: The life of a lesbian nun in Renaissance Italy.* New York: Oxford University Press.

Brown, P. (1988). *The body and society: Men, women and sexual renunciation in early Christianity.* New York: Columbia University Press.

Bruni, F., & Burkett, E. (2002). *A gospel of shame: Children, sexual abuse and the Catholic Church.* New York: Penguin.

Bullough, V. L. (1990). History in adult human sexual behavior with children and adolescents in western societies. In J.R. Feierman (Ed.), *Pedophilia: Biosocial Dimensions* (pp. 69-90). New York: Springer-Verlag.

Carnes, P. J. (1991). *Don't call it love: Recovery from sexual addiction.* New York: Bantam Books.

Catholic League for Religious and Civil Rights. (2004). Sexual abuse in social context: Catholic clergy and other professionals. <www.catholicleague.org>

Cauce, A. M., Tyler, K. A., & Whitbeck, L. B. (2004). Maltreatment and victimization in homeless adolescents: Out of the frying pan and into the fire. *The Prevention Researcher, 11,* 12-14.

Chibnall, J. T., Wolf, A., & Duckro, P. N. (1998). A national survey of the sexual trauma experiences of Catholic nuns. *Review of Religious Research, 40,* 142-167.

Cleary, J. S., Schmieler, C. R., Parascenzo, L. C., & Ambrosio, N. (1994). Sexual harassment of college students: Implications for campus health promotion. *Journal of American College Health, 43,* 3-11.

Cole, W. (1992). Incest perpetrators: their assessment and treatment. *Clinical Forensic Psychiatry, 15,* 689-101.

Cozzens, D. (2002). *Sacred silence: Denial and the crisis in the church.* Collegeville, MN: Liturgical Press.

Curb, R., & Manahan, N. (Eds.) (1985). *Lesbian nuns: Breaking silence.* Tallahassee, FL: Naiad Press.

Darke, J. L. (1990). Sexual aggression: Achieving power through humiliation. In W. L. Marshall, D. R. Laws, & H. E. Barbaree (Eds.), *Handbook of sexual assault: Issues, theories, and treatment of the offender* (pp. 55-72). New York: Plenum Press.

Donn, J., & Ritter, M. (2002, April 14). Sex abuse researchers, therapists fault church and society [Electronic version]. *The Standard-Times*, p. B1.

Donovan, G. (2002, November 1). Women religious address abuse within their ranks [Electronic version]. *National Catholic Reporter.* <natcath.org>

Donovan, G. (2003, January 10). Psychologists dispute Ratzinger's figures [Electronic version]. *National Catholic Reporter.* <natcath.org>

Doyle, T. P. (2003). Roman Catholic clericalism, religious duress, and clergy sexual abuse. *Pastoral Psychology, 51,* 189-231.

Doyle, T. P., Sipe, A. W. R., & Wall, P. J. (2006). *Sex, priests, and secret codes: The Catholic Church's 2,000-year paper trail of sexual abuse.* Los Angeles, Volt Press.

Dreher, R. (2002). The gay question: An issue that cannot be ignored. In P. Thigpen (Ed.), *Shaken by scandals: Catholics speak out about priests' sexual abuse* (pp. 67-76). Ann Arbor, MI: Servant Publications.

Elliott, D. M. (1994). The impact of Christian faith on the prevalence and sequelae of sexual abuse. *Journal of Interpersonal Violence, 9,* 95-108.

Elliott, M. (1994). What survivors tell us: An overview. In M. Elliott (Ed.), *Female sexual abuse of children* (pp. 5-13). New York: Guilford Press.

Falkenhain, M. A., Ducro, P. N., Hughes, H. M., Rossetti, S. J., & Gfeller, J. D. (1999). Cluster analysis of child sexual offenders: A validation with Roman Catholic priests and brothers. *Sexual Addiction & Compulsivity, 6,* 317-336.

Faulkner, A. H., & Cranston, K. (1998). Correlates of same-sex sexual behavior in a random sample of Massachusetts high school students. *American Journal of Public Health, 88,* 262-266.

Federal Bureau of Investigation (1995). Uniform Crime Reports: Number of arrests for forcible rape and other sex offenses, 1980-95. In L. A. Greenfeld (1997) *Sex offenses and offenders: An analysis of the data on rape and sexual assault* (BJS report, NCJ Publication No. 163392, p. 8). Washington, DC: U.S. Department of Justice.

Feierman, J. R. (Ed.). (1990). *Pedophilia: Biosocial dimensions.* New York: Springer-Verlag.

Finkelhor, D. (1984). *Child sexual abuse: New theory and research.* New York: The Free Press.

Fox-Genovese, E. (2003). Crisis in the church, church in crisis? *Society, 40*(3), 10-12.

Francis, P. C., & Turner, N. R. (1995). Sexual misconduct within the Christian church: Who are the perpetrators and those they victimize? *Counseling and Values, 39,* 218-227.

Friedrich, W. N. (1990). *Psychotherapy of sexually abused children and their families.* New York: W. W. Norton.

Gabbard, G. O. (1995). Psychotherapists who transgress sexual boundaries with patients. In J. C. Gonsiorek (Ed.), *Breach of trust: Sexual exploitation by health care professionals and clergy* (pp.133-144). Thousand Oaks, CA: Sage Publications.

Garland, R. J., & Dougher, M. J. (1990). The abused/abuser hypothesis of child sexual abuse: Critical review of theory and research. In J. R. Feierman (Ed.), *Pedophilia: Biosocial dimensions* (pp. 488-509). New York: Springer-Verlag.

Gartner, R. B. (1999). *Betrayed as boys: Psychodynamic treatment of sexually abused men.* New York: Guilford Press.

Gebhard, P. H., Gagnon, J. H., Pomeroy, W. B., & Christenson, C. V. (1965). *Sex offenders: An analysis of types.* New York: Harper & Row.

Gerard, S. M., Jobes, D., & Cimbolic, P. (2003). A Rorschach study of interpersonal disturbance in priest child molestors. *Sexual Addiction & Compulsivity, 10,* 53-66.

Gonsiorek, J. C. (1995). Assessment for rehabilitation of exploitative health care professionals and clergy. In J. C. Gonsiorek (Ed.), *Breach of trust: Sexual exploitation by health care professionals and clergy* (pp.145-162). Thousand Oaks, CA: Sage Publications.

Gonzalez, J. L. (1971). *A history of Christian thought, vol. 2: From Augustine to the eve of the Reformation.* Nashville: Abingdon Press.

Greeley, A. M. (2004). *Priests: A calling in crisis.* Chicago: University of Chicago Press.

Greenfeld, L. A. (1997). *Sex offenses and offenders: An analysis of data on rape and sexual assault.* (BJS report, NCJ Publication No. 163392, p. 8). Washington, DC: U.S. Department of Justice.

Hartigan, J. D. (2003). More reforms are needed. *Society, 40*(3), 13-15.

Hastings, A. S. (1994). *From generation to generation: understanding sexual attraction to children.* Gretna, LA: Wellness Institute.

Haywood, T. W., Kravitz, H. M., Grossman, L. S., Wasyliw, O. E., & Hardy, D. W. (1996). Psychological aspects of sexual functioning among cleric and noncleric alleged sex offenders. *Child Abuse and Neglect, 20,* 527-536.

Haywood, T. W., Kravitz, H. M., Wasyliw, O. E., Goldberg, J. & Cavanaugh, J. L. (1996). Cycle of abuse and psychopathology in cleric and noncleric molesters of children and adolescents. *Child Abuse and Neglect, 20,* 1233-1243.

Headington, G. L. (1997). *A guide to recovery for fallen pastors: The journey back from sexual misconduct.* Ann Arbor, MI: UMI Dissertation Services.

Herman, J. L. (1990). Sex offenders: A feminist perspective. In W. L. Marshall, D. R. Laws, & H. E. Barbaree (Eds.), *Handbook of sexual assault: Issues, theories, and treatment of the offender* (pp. 177-194). New York: Plenum Press.

Higson, F. (Producer) & Mullan, P. (Writer/Director). (2003). *The Magdelene Sisters* [Motion picture]. United States: Miramax Films.

Hill, A. (1995). *Habits of sin: An expose of nuns who sexually abuse children and each other.* Philadelphia: Xlibris Corporation.

Hislop, J. (2001). *Female sex offenders: What therapists, law enforcement and child protective services need to know.* Ravensdale, WA: Issues Press.

Hucker, S. J., & Bain, J. (1990). Androgenic hormones and sexual assault. In W. L. Marshall, D. R. Laws, & H. E. Barbaree (Eds.), *Handbook of sexual assault: Issues, theories, and treatment of the offender* (pp. 93-102). New York: Plenum Press.

Imbens, A., & Jonkers, I. (1992). *Christianity and incest.* Minneapolis: Fortress Press. (Original work published 1985 as *Godsdient en incest*).

Jenkins, P. (1996). *Pedophiles and priests: Anatomy of a contemporary crisis.* New York: Oxford University Press.

Jennings, K. T. (1994). Female child molesters: A review of the literature. In M. Elliott (Ed.), *Female sexual abuse of children* (pp. 219-234). New York: Guilford Press.

Jenny, C., Roesler, T. A., & Poyer, K. L. (1994). Are children at risk for sexual abuse by homosexuals? [Abstract]. *Pediatrics, 94,* 41-44.

John Jay College of Criminal Justice (2004). *The nature and scope of the problem of sexual abuse of minors by Catholic priests and deacons in the United States.* Washington, DC: U.S. Conference of Catholic Bishops.

Kaiser, H. (1996). Clergy sexual abuse in U.S. mainline churches, *American Studies International, 34,* 30-42.

Kaplan, H. S. (1974). *The new sex therapy.* New York: Brunner/Mazel.

Kemp, A. (1998). *Abuse in the family: An introduction.* Pacific Grove, CA: Brooks/Cole Publishing Company.

Kennedy, E. (2002). *The unhealed wound: The church and human sexuality.* New York: St. Martin's Griffin.

Kimball, C., & Golding, J. (2004). Adolescent maltreatment: an overview of the research. *The Prevention Researcher, 11,* 3-6.

Knight, R. A., & Prentky, R. A. (1990). Classifying sexual offenders: The development and corroboration of taxonomic models. In W. L. Marshall, D. R. Laws, & H. E. Barbaree (Eds.), *Handbook of sexual assault: Issues, theories, and treatment of the offender* (pp. 23-52). New York: Plenum Press.

Lamb, D. H., & Catanzaro, S. J. (1998). Sexual and nonsexual boundary violations involving psychologists, clients, supervisees, and students: Implications for professional practice. *Professional Psychology Research and Practice, 29,* 498-503.

Langan, P. A., Schmitt, E. L., & Durose, M. R. (2003). *Recidivism of sex offenders released from prison in 1994.* (BJS report, NCJ Publication No. 198281). Washington, DC: U.S. Department of Justice.

Langevin, R. (Ed.). (1985). *Erotic preference, gender identity, and aggression in men: New research studies.* Hillsdale, NJ: Lawrence Erlbaum Associates.

Langevin, R. (1990). Sexual anomalies and the brain. In W. L. Marshall, D. R. Laws, & H. E. Barbaree (Eds.), *Handbook of sexual assault: Issues, theories, and treatment of the offender* (pp. 103-114). New York: Plenum Press.

Langevin, R., Curnoe, S., & Bain, J. (2000). A study of clerics who commit sexual offenses: Are they different from other sex offenders? *Child Abuse and Neglect, 24,* 535-545.

Laws, D. R., & Marshall, W. L. (1990). A conditioning theory of the etiology and maintenance of deviant sexual preference and behavior. In W. L. Marshall, D. R. Laws, & H. E. Barbaree (Eds.), *Handbook of sexual assault: Issues, theories, and treatment of the offender* (pp. 209-230). New York: Plenum Press.

Loftus, J. A. (1999). Sexuality in priesthood: Noli me tangere. In T. G. Plante (Ed.), *Bless me father for I have sinned: Perspectives on sexual abuse committed by Roman Catholic priests* (pp. 7-19). Westport, CT: Praeger.

Loftus, J. A., & Camargo, R. J. (1993). Treating the clergy. *Annals of Sex Research, 6,* 287-303.

Lothstein, L. (1999). Neuropsychological findings in clergy who sexually abuse. In T. G. Plante (Ed.), *Bless me father for I have sinned: Perspectives on sexual abuse committed by Roman Catholic priests* (pp. 59-86). Westport, CT: Praeger.

Lowery, M. (2002). A moment of grace for the church: The dynamic renewal of seminary culture. In P. Thigpen (Ed.), *Shaken by scandals: Catholics speak out about priests' sexual abuse* (pp. 43-53). Ann Arbor, MI: Servant Publications.

Maddock, J. W., & Larson, N. R. (1995). *Incestuous families: An ecological approach to understanding and treatment.* New York: W.W. Norton.

Maher, M. J. S. (2001). *Being gay and lesbian in a Catholic high school: Beyond the uniform.* Binghamton, NY: The Haworth Press.

Markham, D. J. (2002). Some facts about women religious and child abuse. *Covenant*, September, 3.

Markham, D. J., & Mikail, S. F. (2004). Perpetrators of clergy abuse of minors: Insights from attachment theory. In T. G. Plante (Ed.), *Sin against the innocents: Sexual abuse by priests and the role of the Catholic Church* (pp. 101-114). Westport, CT: Praeger.

Matthews, J. K. (1994). Working with female sexual abusers. In M. Elliott (Ed.), *Female sexual abuse of children* (pp. 57-73). New York: Guilford Press.

Moller, D. (2003, March 7). Sexual assaults raise troubling questions [Electronic version]. *The Nevada City Union.* <theunion.com>

Murrin, M. R., & Laws, D. R. (1990). The influence of pornography on sexual crimes. In W. L. Marshall, D. R. Laws, & H. E. Barbaree (Eds.), *Handbook of sexual assault: Issues, theories, and treatment of the offender* (pp. 73-92). New York: Plenum Press.

National Institute of Mental Health (2004). *Suicide facts and statistics.* Bethesda, MD: U.S. Department of Health and Human Services. <www.nimh.nih.gov>

National Review Board for the Protection of Children and Young People (2004). *A report on the crisis in the Catholic Church in the United States.* Washington, DC: U.S. Conference of Catholic Bishops.

Orlandis, J. (1985). *A short history of the Catholic Church.* (M. Adams, Trans.). Dublin: Four Courts Press.

Pawlaczyk, G. (2002, August 31). O'Fallon nun faced abuse complaint at Louisiana school. *Belleville News Democrat,* 1A-2A.

Plante, T. (1999). Conclusion: Sexual abuse committed by Roman Catholic priests: Current status, future objectives. In T. Plante (Ed.) *Bless me father for I have sinned: Perspectives on sexual abuse committed by Roman Catholic priests* (pp. 171-177). Westport, CT: Praeger Publishers.

Plante, T. (2002). A perspective on clergy sexual abuse. <www.psywww.com/relig/plante.html>

Plante, T. G., Manuel, G., & Bryant, C. (1996). Personality and cognitive functioning among hospitalized sexual offending Roman Catholic priests [Abstract]. *Pastoral Psychology, 45,* 129-139.

Pope, K. S. (2001). Sex between therapists and clients. In J. Worell (Ed.) *Encyclopedia of women and gender: Sex similarities and differences and the impact of society on gender.* San Diego: Academic Press. <kspope.com>

Pope, K. S., Levenson, H., & Schover, L. R. (1979). Sexual intimacy in training: Results and implications of a national survey. *American Psychologist, 34,* 682-689. <kspope.com>

Pope, K. S., & Vetter, V. A. (1991). Prior therapist-patient sexual involvement among patients seen by psychologists. *Psychotherapy, 28*(3), 429-438. <kspope.com>

Prendergast, W. E. (1993). *The merry-go-round of sexual abuse: Identifying and treating survivors.* Binghamton, NY: The Haworth Press.

Prendergast, W. E. (2004). *Treating sex offenders: A guide to clinical practice with adults, clerics, children, and adolescents.* Binghamton, NY: The Haworth Press.

Price, S. (1995). Enhancing positive spirituality, sex offenders and pastoral care. In B. K. Schwartz & H. R. Cellini (Eds.), *The sex offender: Corrections, treatment and legal practice.* Kingston, NJ: Civic Research Institute.

Proctor, C. D., & Groze, V. K. (1994). Risk factors for suicide among gay, lesbian, and bisexual youths. *Social Work, 39,* 504-513.

Pryor, D. W. (1996). *Unspeakable acts: Why men sexually abuse children.* New York: New York University Press.

Putnam, F. W. (2003). Ten-year research update review: Child sexual abuse. *Journal of the American Academy of Child and Adolescent Psychiatry, 42,* 269-278.

Rediger, G. L. (1990). *Ministry and sexuality: Cases, counseling, and care.* Minneapolis: Fortress Press.

Rediger, G. L. (2003). *Beyond the scandals: A guide to healthy sexuality for clergy.* Minneapolis: Fortress Press.

Rodgers, A. (2004, February 23). Bishops' sex abuse report due Friday: Study will be the first to document all cases [Electronic version]. *Pittsburgh Post-Gazette.* <www.post-gazette.com>

Rom, L. (2002a, August 7). Devotion and deceit. *The Times of Acadiana,* 18-22.

Rom, L. (2002b, November 1). Victim, experts tell of abuse by nuns [Electronic version]. *National Catholic Reporter.* <natcath.org>

Rom, L. (2002c, August 13,). Vows of silence. *The Gambit Weekly,* 19-25.

Rossetti, S. J. (1995). The impact of child sexual abuse on attitudes toward God and the Catholic Church. *Child Abuse and Neglect, 19,* 1469-1481.

Rossetti, S. J. (1996). *A tragic grace.* Collegeville, MN: Liturgical Press.

Rossetti, S. J. (2002). The Catholic Church and child sexual abuse. *America,* April, 8-15.

Rudin, M. M., Zalewski, C., & Bodmer-Turner, J. (1995). Characteristics of child sexual abuse victims according to perpetrator gender [Abstract]. *Child Abuse and Neglect, 19,* 963-973.

Saradjian, A., & Nobus, D. (2003). Cognitive distortions of religious professionals who sexually abuse children. *Journal of Interpersonal Violence, 18,* 905-923.

Schore, A. N. (2003). Early relational trauma, disorganized attachment, and the development of a predisposition to violence. In M. F. Solomon & D. J. Siegel

(Eds.), *Healing trauma: Attachment, mind, body, and brain* (pp. 107-167). New York: W.W. Norton.

Schwartz, B. K. (1995). Theories of sex offenses. In B. K. Schwartz & H. R. Cellini (Eds.). *The sex offender: Corrections, treatment and legal practice* (pp. 2-2-2-32). Kingston, NJ: Civic Research Institute.

Schwartz, B. K., & Cellini, H. R. (1995). Female sex offenders. In B. K. Schwartz & H. R. Cellini (Eds.), *The sex offender: Corrections, treatment and legal practice* (pp. 5-1-5-22). Kingston, NJ: Civic Research Institute.

Segal, Z. V., & Stermac, L. E. (1990). The role of cognition in sexual assault. In W. L. Marshall, D. R. Laws, & H. E. Barbaree (Eds.), *Handbook of sexual assault: Issues, theories, and treatment of the offender* (pp. 161-174). New York: Plenum Press.

Shakeshaft, C. (2003). Educator Sexual Abuse. *Hofstra Horizons*, Spring, 10-13.

Shakeshaft, C. (2004). *Educator sexual misconduct: A synthesis of existing literature*. Washington, DC: U.S. Department of Education.

Sherr, R. (1991). A canon, a choirboy, and homosexuality in late sixteenth-century Italy: A case study [Abstract]. *Journal of Homosexuality, 21,* 1-22.

Siegel, D. J. (2003). An interpersonal neurobiology of psychotherapy: The developing mind and the resolution of trauma. In M. F. Solomon & D. J. Siegel (Eds.), *Healing trauma: Attachment, mind, body, and brain* (pp. 1-56). New York: W.W. Norton.

Simpkinson, A. A. (1996). Soul betrayal. *Common Boundary,* November/December. <www.advocateweb.org>

Sipe, A. W. R. (1995). *Sex, priests, and power: Anatomy of a crisis.* New York: Brunner/Mazel.

Sipe, A. W. R. (2003). *Celibacy in crisis: A secret world revisited.* New York: Brunner-Routledge.

Smith, C. A., Thornberry, T. P., & Ireland, T. O. (2004). Adolescent maltreatment and its impact: Timing matters. *The Prevention Researcher, 11,* 7-11.

Snyder, H. N. (2000). *Sexual assault of young children as reported to law enforcement: Victim, incident and offender characteristics* (NCJ Publication No. 182990). Washington, DC: U.S. Department of Justice.

Stermac, L. E., Segal, Z. V., & Gillis, R. (1990). Social and cultural factors in sexual assault. In W. L. Marshall, D. R. Laws, & H. E. Barbaree (Eds.), *Handbook of sexual assault: Issues, theories, and treatment of the offender* (pp. 143-160). New York: Plenum Press.

Steward, D. S., & Driskill, J. (1991). Listening to young children tell about their pain. *Religious Education, 86,* 441-454.

Thorman, G. (1983). *Incestuous families.* Springfield, IL: Charles C Thomas.

U.S. Census Bureau (2003). *Statistical Abstracts of the United States* (No. 11: Resident population by age and sex: 1980-2002). Washington, DC: U.S. Government Printing Office.

U.S. Census Bureau (2003). *Statistical Abstracts of the United States* (No. 315: Reporting rape and sexual assault to police and medical attention: 1992 to 2000). Washington, DC: U.S. Government Printing Office.

U.S. Census Bureau (2003). *Statistical Abstracts of the United States* (No. HS-23. Crimes and crime rates by type of offense: 1960 to 2002). Washington, DC: U.S. Government Printing Office.

U.S. Conference of Catholic Bishops (2002). *Charter for the Protection of Children and Young People.* Washington, DC: Author.

van der Kolk, B. A. (2003). Posttraumatic stress disorder and the nature of trauma. In M. F. Solomon & D. J. Siegel (Eds.), *Healing trauma: Attachment, mind, body, and brain* (pp. 168-195). New York: W. W. Norton.

Vatican Congregation for the Doctrine of the Faith (1994). *Catechism of the Catholic Church.* Rome: Author.

Wakefield, H., Rogers, M., & Underwager, R. (1990). Female sexual abusers: A theory of loss. *Institute for Psychological Therapies, 2.* <Ipt-forensics.com/journal>

Ward, T., Hudson, S. M., & McCormack, J. (1997). Attachment style, intimacy deficits, and sexual offending. In B. K. Schwartz & H. R. Cellini (Eds.), *The sex offender: New insights, treatment innovations and legal developments,* Vol. 2 (pp. 2-1-2-2-14). Kingston, NJ: Civic Research Institute.

White, W. L. (1995). A systems perspective on sexual exploitation of clients by professional helpers. In J. C. Gonsiorek (Ed.), *Breach of trust: Sexual exploitation by health care professionals and clergy* (pp. 176-192). Thousand Oaks, CA: Sage Publications.

Williams, L. M., & Finkelhor, D. (1990). The characteristics of incestuous fathers: A review of recent studies. In W. L. Marshall, D. R. Laws, & H. E. Barbaree (Eds.), *Handbook of sexual assault: Issues, theories, and treatment of the offender* (pp. 231-255). New York: Plenum Press.

Williams-Morris, R. (1994). Incest and conservative family values. *Adventist Today*, January–February. <www.atoday.com>

Wills, G. (2000). *Papal sin: Structures of deceit.* New York: Doubleday.

Zoll, R. (2002, March 22). Researchers caution Catholic Church against targeting gays in priest abuse crisis. *Associated Press,* 1.

Index

Page numbers followed by the letter "f" indicate figures; those followed by the letter "t" indicate tables.

doi:10.1300/5633_08